T0149413

CONFESSIONS

OF A MELBOURNE COMMUTER

RENELO DRUMMER

BALBOA.
PRESS

A DIVISION OF HAY HOUSE

Balboa Press books may be ordered through booksellers or by contacting:

Balboa Press
A Division of Hay House
1663 Liberty Drive
Bloomington, IN 47403
www.balboapress.com.au
1 (877) 407-4847

Print information available on the last page.

ISBN: 978-1-5043-0681-2 (sc)
ISBN: 978-1-5043-0682-9 (e)

Balboa Press rev. date: 03/06/2017

This book is dedicated to my Creator

THANK YOU

To all my family and friends including:

Matt Lewis
Rhett Dale
Mary Mills
Samuel Peque
Renelo Zammit
Abraham Peque

And also to the:

Melbourne commuters
who made my daily commute interesting.

THE JOURNEY

It was July 2014. I was alone and cold. By this time, I had quit my job to work on the accounting business that I've been doing on the weekends. For the first couple of weeks, it was fantastic. I had all the time to work on my clients. I had also more time to think about what I wanted to do and the projects I wanted to start.

I enjoyed having total control of my schedule. I could schedule things I wanted to do and events I wanted to attend. It was fantastic.

After a few weeks of doing my own thing, I started to feel isolated. There were times that I wanted to bounce some ideas off someone but there was no one. It was just me working on my laptop all day. For the first time after I quit my job, I missed the people I used to work with. I missed working with a team.

Then I thought about looking for a job somewhere in the city. A role that is team-oriented. I sent my resume to an agency. I received a call from them not long after that. They found me a role in the south side of the city (Melbourne) that they thought I might be interested in. I went for the interview. Shortly after that they called me in again for another interview.

After about a week, the agency rang me to say that I got the job. It all happened so fast that I almost didn't have time to think about whether this was the job I was looking for. I accepted the offer to join the company and started the following week.

THE IDEA

It's been a while since I used to catch the train to the city for work. When I accepted the new job, I knew that I would be commuting to work every day. Pictures of people doing different things on the train flashed in my mind. Yelling, chatting, sneezing, staring at other people (crap!), picking their noses (what the!), scratching their _____ (unbelievable!), among others.

The first week was challenging as I tried to change my routine and adjust to the new environment. The second week was getting better. I quickly adjusted. I set up a new routine. It was during this time that this idea to write this book came about.

I noticed other passengers do strange things on the train. A lot crazier than I initially thought. The conversations people were having, became more interesting. That's when I decided to create a travel diary on my phone and started writing down what I see and hear on the train and tram.

Each entry has its own title based on the highlights for that day. To give you an example, one of the entries is called *Phlegm*. There was this guy who coughed out his phlegm and spat it out on the train floor in front of another passenger. Another example is entitled *B.O.* A guy was standing next to me, put on his surgical mask and looked at me. I thought he was sending me a message that I had B.O. I was pretty sure I showered that morning.

THE LESSON

During the writing of this travel diary, I realised that I was trying to force myself to be someone I'm not. I don't like watching other people's activities on the train. I certainly don't like to listen to other people's conversations. I was doing it because I promised myself to complete this project. I don't want to start something that I can't finish, unless there is any plausible excuse. About halfway through this project, I noticed that I became more observant to little things, sensitive to quiet conversations and easily distracted by pretty women.

I thought about giving up towards the end of the project. In fact, I thought about it quite a lot that I couldn't sleep for some nights. In the end, I decided that I didn't want to break the promise I made to myself. I stuck to the initial plan and completed the project. That is why you are reading this book right now.

A friend told me that in any given situation, there will be benefits and drawbacks. The truth, however, of any experience is not what you go through but rather how you perceive it. (Thanks Matt).

When he said this to me, I realised that because of this book project, I discovered more things about myself that I would not have known otherwise. I realised that I have more discipline than I thought. I learned how to appreciate beauty in its true sense, not as a result of testosterone. I learned how to be more considerate to other people. I developed incredible levels of patience and forgiveness during my journey and towards the completion of this project.

Lastly, I discovered more of my weaknesses as a human being. I was guilty of pointing out other people's shortcomings that I overlooked my own. I realised that people are quick to judge or label other people just because they are different, both in physical features and ideology.

I am not perfect. I made mistakes. I know.

Now, I'm a better person because of this project.

Thank you.

Renelo Drummer

THIS CHAPTER IS DEDICATED TO
ALL MELBOURNE COMMUTERS

SEPTEMBER 2014

29th, Monday

My first seat

After three weeks of commuting, I finally got a seat on the train from my station.

I can read a book comfortably now. Yes!

When I started reading, this crazy guy sitting next to me started dozing off. He leaned his head on my shoulder. I noticed some dandruff. I could not believe it!

What do I do? Should I keep my cool or play the 'nasty card'?

Fortunately for him, I was in a good mood this morning and had a few drops of patience to spare. Besides it's the first entry to my diary and I didn't want to paint a scene of bruises and blood, broken ribs and black eyes. He decided to come back to life before my patience ran out.

I was happy again. And because it is spring time and I had my stylish spring jacket on, I was happier.

When I was waiting for my tram on Collins Street, the street cleaner was cleaning the tram tracks with his ride-on sweeper and we all covered our mouths for three minutes. It felt like it was going on forever.

Why couldn't he do it during office hours, while people are inside their offices?

After he finished cleaning our section of the tram stop, my shirt was covered in dust. Just nice!

When I got on the tram, I stood next to a cute gal listening to her music. I felt happy again. Well, that happiness lasted for a minute until this guy tried to squeeze himself onto the tram steps and he stood between me and the pretty gal.

It was crazy! 'C'mon man, just wait for the next tram,' I felt like saying it to him.

I got off my tram stop; which was just outside McDonald's. I needed my medium soy cappuccino before work.

End of the day. I finished work late at my new job. The tram was delayed by three minutes which felt like forever.

I dropped by the city to get some dinner. While I was walking on Swanston Street, a guy who was wearing a shirt with an Asian restaurant logo cut me off and tried to elbow me.

What the heck was that about?

30th, Tuesday

Little things

It's the second day in a row for me to get a seat on the train from my station. I sat next to a good-looking, well-dressed lady. It was the perfect seat of me on a perfect 24°C morning.

Coming out of the train station was a little crazy. Although there were a lot of things and noises around me, I wasn't really bothered by them. I could still feel peace within me. This made me realise that sometimes happiness is just enjoying the little things. It doesn't need to be grand like winning a million dollars in the lotto or an inheritance from a long lost uncle who moved to Denmark.

Back to simple things. From now on, every time I feel down or discouraged, I will remind myself of those little things I enjoy—my favourite spring jacket, the good weather, that smile from a fellow commuter, that funny tram driver and or your coffee made by that girl you have a crush on at McDonald's.

Remember those little things.

OCTOBER 2014

1ˢᵗ, Wednesday

Newbies

There were two teenage girls on the train who seemed lost. They were trying to figure out what train they were on and how to get to their destination by looking at the train network map. Though, I would assume that most people have smartphones these days, particularly young people. These days, there is almost no excuse to get lost. It only takes a few taps to look up an address on your phone.

2ⁿᵈ, Thursday

Reading

I didn't get a seat on the train. I was hoping to get one because I was early. Anyway, I stood next to this cute Asian girl who was reading her iPad. She wasn't holding onto anything. It's amazing how she kept her balance on a moving train and was still able to read. Normally, when I read while standing on the train or tram, one hand always holds a rail to keep my balance. This also saves me from a potential embarrassing fall which actually happened to me before. Trust me, it was not a pleasant experience.

I looked around the train and people were all reading. So I pulled out my Seth Godin book and continued from where I stopped the other day. The chapter was about spreading ideas like a virus.

I read an article on *mX* that commuting made people more productive. During travel, they read more, make phone calls, prepare for exams and do their homework. I totally agree with that because that's what I've been doing. I did some calculations to work out how much time is saved or spent on travelling or driving. Take driving for example. It takes an hour to drive to work and another from work to home. That's two hours every day. And that's even conservative because there are days when traffic is so bad (more like every day anyway!). If you work five days a week, you would spend ten hours wasted on driving. Multiply that by 52 weeks to get 520 hours in a year. That's equivalent to 65 working days which is over two months. That is crazy! Absolutely unbelievable!

Imagine what you can do with those hours. I can probably finish reading a few books or write another one. Perhaps, complete a song-writing course. Now, I'm thinking to take up a law degree.

3rd, Friday

Chillax

It's Friday and it was an early start for me to host a community radio program. I got up at 5 A.M. to get ready, and drove to the train station to catch the 6:05 A.M. train. My radio program starts at 7 A.M.

When I got up this morning, there was a voice inside my head telling me to skip the radio and to go back to bed. But then these pictures of success, community work and helping kids kept flashing in my mind. So I forced myself to get up. I went to shower, put my clothes on and rushed to catch my train. I made it the radio station just right on time. My co-broadcaster was there.

I'm glad that he shows up every Friday morning. Community radio broadcasters don't get paid to do this that's why I admire everyone's dedication and love for community radio.

I try to take it easy on Fridays. I chillax (chill and relax). So I went to the DFO on Spencer Street to check out some books to buy. Every week I try to finish a book so that by Friday I'm ready to buy a new one. This means that I need to get a reasonably thin book that I can finish in five days.

It is going be a lot of reading for me on the train, tram, McDonald's and Starbucks (TTMS).

6th, Monday

Britney

This girl on the train who was talking to her friend kept going on and on about her holidays and how absolute fun it was. She talked the whole time I was on the train. It was almost impossible to listen to. Unfortunately for me, I didn't bring my headphones today so I was stuck listening to this girl.

Great! It's going to be live and loud train music.

During this time of difficulty, I needed inspiration. All I could think of was Britney Spears' *Baby One More Time*. I had to play it in my head and looped it four times which was the whole time this girl was talking.

I don't know if I want to laugh or be annoyed but one thing I can take from this is that when you talk to someone in public, don't talk so loudly that everyone can hear. Imagine if you're a guy and you're talking to your female friend about how your girlfriend dumped you because you cheated. Then you walked away still dancing with the beat in your Hawaiian shirt. Or if you're a girl and you're talking to your friend about how your cat plays with your underwear in the laundry.

Keep personal things personal. Don't let the world know about it.

7th, Tuesday

Plus size

I sat next to a plus size lady. I don't know if it's politically correct to say this but please bear with me. I can probably use large or solid instead of plus size. But when I sat there all I could think of was '_____'.

It's been a huge day as well at work. It's only been a few weeks from when I started and we've already been doing a few projects.

I found out something today when you live in areas classified as zone 2. When you catch tram 109 from Balwyn or Box Hill, Zone 1 ticket is all you need although they are classified as Zone 2 areas. Areas after Balwyn towards the city are classified as Zone 1. But if you catch the train instead of tram from Balwyn/Canterbury or Box Hill, you will need both Zones 1 and 2 ticket. I don't get the logic behind all of that but at least I know that if I'm not in a hurry I can catch the tram and only use a Zone 1 ticket. Thanks to the Metro staff at Southern Cross station who told me this, although I wasn't totally convinced.

Note: They merged both zones 1 and 2 in January 2015 for price purposes. You buy a ticket for zones 1 and 2 for the price of one.

8th, Wednesday

First carriage

I got on the first carriage of the train. I'm trying to make this a habit now to be on the first carriage. There are certain benefits, at least for me, if you are on the first carriage. First, I can exit the station quicker because I will be closer to the exit points. Second, there is a better chance that you will get a seat. Why? Because most people don't normally wait right at the end of the platform where the first carriage stops. Most of them wait for the middle carriage.

Furthermore, in case of distress, it's easier to get the driver's attention because you'll be just behind the driver's cabin.

9th, Thursday

Somebody That I Used to Know

Today was inspiring, but also annoying.

Let me start with the annoying part. I was rushing to catch my train when a lady came out of nowhere and cut me off when I was about to step on the escalator at Southern Cross Station. She seemed completely oblivious to what she did. I had every reason to get angry. Instead, I didn't let myself get affected or the rest of my day. She just reminded me of Gotye's *Somebody That I Used to Know* with the line that says, 'but you didn't have to cut me off.

Unbelievable!

That's okay. At least, when I got to the platform, I saw something sweet.

I saw two friends (male and female) talking who seemed like they haven't seen each other for a long time. As they hugged each other, it reminded me of my high school friends. High school days are one of my most memorable moments. I just thought friendships are one of the most beautiful things that we sometimes take for granted, myself included. It's the cutest thing.

10th, Friday

Wrong

Today was quite an eventful one. Oh my, where do I start?

Well, when I got on the train this morning, a guy was sitting on one of the side seats just behind the driver's cabin. It normally sits two people but this guy put his phone and other personal things on the seat so he basically occupied the whole two-seater. The rest of the passengers are squeezing in just to be on that train. What's even funnier was a lady got on from Surrey Hills and stood in front of him. Then she looked at him possible trying to send the message that she might want a seat. He didn't move a muscle. Unbelievable!

During all this time, I was standing and I could feel my sweat in my stylish winter jacket. I wanted to take it off but it was just too packed on the train to even move my arms. Being stylish just goes out the window when you're full of sweat. It's not funny!

After work I was in such a rush to get home that I caught the wrong train. I didn't realise it until after we were out of the city loop. Luckily, I realised I could change trains at the next two stations. So I got off Glenferrie Station and waited for the next train. It was my first time at this Station and I wasn't familiar with the platforms. At this point, I started to feel very sleepy so I took a seat. I got up after six minutes when I could hear the train coming. While the train was getting closer, I realised that was going to the other platform.

I missed my train again. Oh my, oh my!

I seriously could sleep right there and then. I just wanted to lie down.

Sigh!

11th, Saturday

Who are you talking to?

It's Saturday. And since I have a monthly myki ticket, my weekend travel is effectively free. I normally park my car in Carlton or Collingwood and catch the tram to the city. I got on the tram and I could hear some guy talking. I turned to look at him but there was no one except himself. I realised he was talking to himself. Mind you, I also do it – talking to myself. I used to ask questions like:

Why did you buy that crazy phone, Renelo?

Crap, how are you going to fix your shoes? Maybe, buy those rubber soles from Daiso?

Where did I put that stupid key?

When are you going to get a girlfriend?

And because questions need answers, I had to respond to my own questions. The answers would be:

That's fine. It's just a backup phone.

Yes, that's right. Daiso! Okay, Renelo, let's go! Giddy-up!

Really? Who's stupid, the key or you?

Girlfriend? Maybe try to ring that girl you met at work the other day.

I remember in my previous jobs, when I talked to myself, people near me didn't know whether to answer or ignore me. Oftentimes, they would respond to me but I was actually just talking to myself. They would feel bad because they thought that I ignored them.

I was on my way home when I decided to have dinner in the city. So I got off the tram and started walking along Swanston Street. There are a lot of Asian restaurants on Swanston. I couldn't decide which one to try – Thai? Chinese? Vietnamese? Japanese? Or maybe McDonalds? I feel blessed to be in Melbourne. In terms of food, there is a never-ending list of choices.

So next time you're in Melbourne and you want to try Asian food, just walk along Swanston Street.

13th, Monday

Rain

Rain greeted me this morning. The fuel gauge on my dashboard hasn't been working properly for the last three days so I didn't actually know if I had enough petrol for the day. It was only a short trip to the station anyway so I was not overly concerned. So I drove. All good!

When I got on the train, I looked towards the back of the carriage. Nothing but people fiddling with their phones. Apparently, a lot more than usual. And I suppose there's not much view outside the window other than the pouring rain. I was pulling out my phone from my pocket when I locked eyes with a girl for a few seconds. Then I looked away.

Man, this is awkward. She was cute. Another lost opportunity. Damn it, Janet!

I continued my reading from last time and after a few minutes I looked away to rest my eyes. Then I looked on my right and I could see someone's belt in front of me.

'Man, am I really this short or is this guy just very tall?' I thought to myself.

I caught the tram home with someone from work. I planned to have dinner in the city but when my colleague got off the tram to catch the train at Southern Cross I suddenly changed my mind and got off the tram too. I jumped off just before the tram driver shut the door, so I was almost squashed.

I was overly tired when I boarded the train so I literally pinched myself so I wouldn't fall asleep. I almost missed my stop the other day because I dozed off and I didn't want it to happen again.

14th, Tuesday

Why me?

I missed my connecting tram by three seconds. I tried my best. I ran like crazy once I got off the train but I still didn't make it.

Why, why me?

I had to wait eight forever minutes for the next tram. When the tram arrived, I was spewing because it was absolutely, incredibly, superfluously, insanely packed. I almost didn't get on the tram because they were passengers standing up to the doors.

Why man, why me?

Luckily, with my minus size body I was able to squeeze in. I don't know how I managed to get into that absolutely, incredibly, superfluously, insanely packed tram.

Tonight I went for a saxophone practice session and then had dinner with a friend. When I got to the shopping centre where I parked my car, I had to pay a late night claim fee of $30.

Why me!

15th, Wednesday

Boring

Today was one those boring days. I read Seth Godin's book on viral marketing on the train. I basically joined a crowd of readers on the train. Boring! When I went to McDonalds to get my caffeine fix, I joined a long boring queue as well. There were boring people everywhere I turned. And that included me.

It was bit boring today as well at work.

Overall, it was basically a boring day.

I'm not normally like this. I don't think I called myself boring before. Today is probably the first time.

16th, Thursday

Candy Crush

When I got on the train, I saw this lady with a very serious face looking down her iPhone. I noticed that she was playing Candy Crush. She reminded me of some of my Facebook friends (both male and female) who sent me Candy Crush invitations. I ignored all of them. You can send me candy but not Candy Crush, please. For those who don't know much about it, Candy Crush is a game where you basically try to match three or more candies of the same colour. When I looked it up YouTube, I came across this guy who had different strategies and tips on how to play it. Some people decided to make playing Candy Crush a career. It's amazing!

So yes, just a reminder to all my Facebook friends: You can send me candies but not Candy Crush please. That would be appreciated!

17th, Friday

JW

While I was waiting for my tram on Collins Street, I locked eyes with a girl wearing a bright-coloured dress. She just got off the tram and I could see her badge, but could not read it. As she was approaching, I was able to read it: *Keep Seeking First God's Kingdom*. Then I realised, she was a member of the Jehovah's Witnesses (JW) church because of the logo. Then more people got off the tram. More and more JW's kept coming out from the next three trams. They were all wearing the same badge. In a matter of seconds the tram stop was populated with JW's.

I must admit they were very well-dressed. They presented themselves well not just by the way they dress but also by the way they smile and walk. I was quite impressed actually. I found out later that their church had a convention that weekend and members from different parts of the world came to Melbourne to attend the event.

When I was a teenager (crap I'm old now!), there was this JW who came to our house and he started talking about salvation and handed out a copy of a brochure or magazine called *Watchtower*. I started reading it and found that the articles were quite interesting. Pretty soon he would bring new issues as soon as they came out. I was in a 'soul-searching' mode back then, looking for a deeper meaning of life, so I read almost all articles of most of the issues. We also discussed a lot of things about history and other religions. I would bombard him with questions and he would always have answers. It was fascinating. I spent almost a year with this guy and I attended a few of their gatherings at their church called *Kingdom Hall*. I also attended a convention which was a massive event for the JW's.

The pressure on me to get converted to be a JW was evident, but deep down in my heart I did not want to become one. There were quite a few things that I didn't agree on including not being able to sing the National Anthem and not being able to celebrate birthdays. Mind you, if you ask my friends, they'll tell you that I don't celebrate my birthday. It's not because I was influenced by the JW's but because I want to measure life against the goals I set last year as opposed to time, if that makes sense. In the end, I listened to my heart and studied Christ instead.

Anyway, after a few long minutes, I was able to get on the tram.

18th, Saturday

JW's again

Yesterday was just the tip of the iceberg. If you read yesterday's entry you know what I mean. I saw a lot of Jehovah's Witnesses (JW's) yesterday but today was just crazy. Everywhere I turn there was a JW. They wore the same badge that said 'Seeking First God's Kingdom.' I also noticed that there were more Customer Service staff at tram stops. I believe they were deployed for the JW's convention this weekend. Apparently, it was a big event for them and many JW's from around the world were expected to gather in Melbourne. I have never seen a never-ending queue of people waiting to board the trams. It was unbelievable!

It was a nice Saturday afternoon to go shopping so I decided to go to DFO on Spencer Street.

Guess, who's at DFO?

More and more JW's.

Over a decade ago I used to read JW's magazine called Watchtower and studied them. Seeing these JW's brought back a lot of memories.

I went to order my soy cappuccino at Coffee Club and there was a long queue.

More JW's.

That's okay. Enjoy your time in Melbourne, guys.

20th, Monday

X-factor

My morning was still full of my weekend memories of packed trams, long queues, badges and JW's. And lots of them.

This plus size lady occupied the whole seat and I was going to sit next to her because I thought, having a minus size body, that I would fit anyway. I was visualising what would happen if I did take a seat — I sit and she moves to the side to give me more room and as I try to squeeze my bottom in. She runs out of room. She gets stuck. I get stuck. That would put both of us in an awkward situation. So I decided to just stand there. In hindsight, it was a good decision.

I've been thinking about the announcement of X-Factor Australia tonight. I couldn't wait for the final results. I am a fan of Marlisa so I wanted her to win. Anyway, both of them are deserving winners.

I am so, so excited!

21st, Tuesday

Happy day

Today is a happy day. Marlisa won last night and I am so happy for her. I voted for her every week and it finally paid off.

This next scene on the train, however, I don't know if I can call it happiness. It's more like 'movieness' if there's such a word.

There's this guy wearing sunglasses that made him look like Hugo Weaving. You know that guy called Mr Smith from *The Matrix* movie. Yes, he definitely looked like him. All he needed was an earpiece so he could start shooting Neo.

There was one thing that happened on the train on my way home that I can perhaps call happiness. I locked eyes with someone. Again! This happened to me many times on the train and I don't like it. Then I tried to look away for a couple of seconds but then we locked eyes again. I then decided to close my eyes and sat there until they announced my station. I guess I might call this awkward scene and not happiness.

22nd, Wednesday

Jogging

I started the day with a 15-minute jog. I felt good and healthy afterwards.

When I got on the train, I didn't get a seat until the train arrived at Melbourne Central station. I thought there was no point sitting down because I was getting off at the next couple of stops.

"Stuff it!" I said.

I took a seat anyway! I think my legs were just tired. Blame it on my jogging.

Someone at work baked some brownies. It was very nice of her. Thank you. You know who you are. We also went to a Malaysian restaurant called Penang Road for lunch.

Today is someone's special day. A guy from a long time ago. I heard he is full of awesomeness. His name can be found in the Book of Whatever, second to the last chapter, just above the page number at the bottom right, on page 177.

The previous paragraph doesn't make sense, right?

Good! That's what it's supposed to be.

By the way, today's early morning jog will probably be the first and the last morning jog. I don't think I can keep getting up at 5 every morning and go for a jog.

23rd, Thursday

Shake it off

I couldn't sleep last night but I didn't want that to affect my plans for today. So I took Taylor Swift's advice about all those unwanted feelings. I shook them off.

I got to the train station feeling energised, ready to start my morning. So I started my morning with something special— reading a book. I know. It's boring.

This book, however, caught my interest when I first picked it up. It's called *Whatcha Gonna Do With That Duck?* It's written by Seth Godin whom I consider a guru in business marketing. I watched his videos. Many of them are interviews of him talking about a whole range of topics from spreading ideas, niche marketing, building a tribe, among others.

When I was reading, Seth mentioned something about barriers to success which immediately reminded me of Roger Bannister. He was the first person to run and break the four-minute barrier. He ran a mile in less than four minutes.

I think these things: the shaking off, Seth Godin and Roger Bannister, were just the things I needed this morning to get me inspired for the day.

We don't need good sleep to get inspired.

Actually, I do!

24th, Friday

Fish

I don't know why I brought my jacket with me this morning when it was warm. Well, I had a choice between a jacket and an umbrella. I went for the jacket. As a Melburnian, part of my routine is to bring either a jacket or an umbrella. With four seasons in one day as they say in Melbourne, it may be sunny in the morning but it could rain in the afternoon. Just hope there won't be any thunderstorms at night. Don't worry, it doesn't hail that much afterwards.

An interesting thing happened to me on the train. I started rolling up my sleeves up for no reason. Then I realised I was just copying the guy standing right next to me.

'I can't believe I'm a copycat,' I thought for a moment.

On the train on my way home, a lady boarded a few stops after Richmond station. She was wearing fishnet stockings. It caught everyone's attention. After a couple of stops, two guys with conspicuous tattoos, boarded the train and stood opposite to the lady with fishnet stockings. They started talking about how they love fish and how they enjoy fishing.

'Oh man, this is embarrassing. I don't want to hear all this stuff,' I sat there thinking as well as feeling sorry and helpless for the lady.

I was thinking I might grab some fish on the way home for dinner.

27th, Monday

Jam-packed

After last night's heavy rains, transportation seems to have been affected. I heard on the radio to expect delays. However, there was one thing they didn't mention—a jam-packed train! You would not believe this, but I literally had to take a deep breath before boarding the train. I usually do this when I go swimming. And this morning I felt like swimming with a lot of people. I didn't need goggles, which is good. Once on the train, I tried to reach for the rail to hold for balance but I couldn't. It was just too crowded. Luckily, I had a good sleep last night, otherwise, I would have fainted.

On the tram to work, I stood next to a lady with conspicuous scars on her arms. I didn't want to look rude but I just couldn't stop looking at them. Then I noticed they were fresh scars. I could feel pain just by looking at them.

Ouch!

28th, Tuesday

Moth balls

My morning didn't start with a jam-packed train like yesterday. When I boarded the train, a very strong smell came from the middle of the carriage. It was a smell of moth balls. It was very strong. I don't know how all the other passengers here lasted this long with this smell.

Why would you bring moth balls with you on the train anyway? What the heck?

That's it. My day was ruined! Crap!

Just joking!

Maybe, I'm not joking.

Whatever man!

29th, Wednesday

Don't smile at me!

Get this. When I got on the train I sat opposite a girl who looked completely miserable. It was like all of heaven fell over her. I tried my best to make a big smile at her to hopefully cheer her up but there was no reaction. I felt like I was making a fool of myself. It didn't matter. I had good intentions. I'm used to rejection anyway. That's probably why I still have zero love life.

On my way home, I was dozing off on the train. I was very tired and I could not remember what was happening around me. Even so, I still tried to keep my eyes open. However, at some point, sleepiness gave in and I was asleep for about 15 minutes. When I opened my eyes, the train had just literally stopped at my station. That was extremely lucky. My night could have ended with a lot of walking.

Whoever or whatever made me open my eyes, thank you!

30th, Thursday

Disability is not weakness but inspiration

A guy on a wheelchair boarded the train. This guy was pretty interesting. He pulled out his MacBook Pro and started working on some design. It looked like he was working on some project. I felt inspired while I was watching him. That we should not let our weaknesses hinder us to keep us from ever pursuing our goals. Then I started to think about my goals and I challenged myself to go even higher.

Later today, I went to the optometrist to have my eyes checked. I don't like optometrists, eyeglasses and the like. I would not have booked an optometrist if I wasn't in pain. So I felt like I didn't have a choice but to book an appointment. Anyway, after the session the result was a prescription for eyeglasses. The optometrist said it was mainly my right eye that needed correction that's why I needed eyeglasses. I could not believe what I heard. I never thought I would wear them in my entire life.

Unbelievable!

I better pick some nice-looking frames at least.

By the way, to that guy in the wheelchair, thank you for inspiring me.

31st, Friday

Mind vs body

It was an early start for me today. I had a radio program at 7 A.M.

'Go back to bed,' my body was telling my mind when I opened my eyes this morning at round 4.45 A.M.

My mind wouldn't listen to my body so I told it to get up and be ready by 5:30 A.M. The ultimatum was implemented. Sometimes we need to command our body to do what we are supposed to do. So I got to the train station early but the parking area was closed. I had to ring the after-hours number so the security guard would open it for me.

My plan to be really early today didn't happen.

After the radio program, I caught up with a fellow broadcaster for breakfast. It was a quick catch-up as I was running late for work. After that I ran towards the tram stop. I was so stressed that I was going to be late for work that I felt like I would have yelled at someone who even smiled at me.

<u>NOVEMBER 2014</u>

3rd, Monday

Piercings

Often, I would quickly plan my day's commute and think about possible titles for the day's diary entry as well as things to watch out for on the train. But not this morning.

Anyway, I jumped on the train and there were empty seats. That didn't help.

Now, who am I going to eavesdrop on?

Then, I realised tomorrow is Melbourne Cup Day. Many people would take the Monday off work (which is today) so they could have a long four-day weekend. That explained why it was quiet on the train this morning.

My tram trip was a different story.

I was on my way to work and someone (or something) caught my attention on the tram—a girl covered with piercings! To be covered with layers of clothing is fine. To be covered with make-up is fine as well. But to be covered with piercings? I don't how to react to that.

It was unreal. Like literally super-duper, unbelievably unreal.

There were piercings on every part of her nose. I didn't even know if she still had her original nose underneath those pieces of metal.

There were also piercings on her lips. How does she even kiss? Or eat Nasi Goreng?

She was wearing a black leather jacket and black earrings. Though I must admit I like how she presented herself, overall.

I could feel the agonising pain of those piercings.

How did she even survive the whole piercing process?

5th, Wednesday

Hello-uh-bye!

It was annoying that my train was redirected to Flinders Street instead of going around the city loop. When the train doors opened I sprinted out of the train, out of the platform and in 27 seconds I was out of the station. I was curious at how fast I was so I looked behind me and there were just people everywhere.

I don't know what the deal was but something must have happened that affected the trains this morning.

I walked from Flinders Street to Collins Street to catch a tram. What happened next was a little bit awkward. When the tram stopped, there was a short delay before the doors opened. When they did open, I saw a familiar face getting off the tram. It was a friend from university a few years ago. I called out her name and she turned around. When she saw my cute face (really?), she called out my name out loud.

We looked at each other for a second, then we said: Hello-uh-bye!

To say hello and bye to an old friend for a couple of seconds is a little awkward.

When I was on the tram I thought, 'I should have stopped to have a quick chat with her.

A few minutes wouldn't hurt. But it's too late now. Crap!

That was probably one of the most awkward moments I have so far. It was awkward because we were good friends during university days. We went to classes together; worked on various projects together and went to lunch together. Not just the two of us but with other friends. And after all these years, we only said hello to each other for two seconds!

6th, Thursday

Couple

Someone caught my attention on the train this morning. A girl who brushed her hair for about 19 minutes. She had been brushing her hair from the time I got on my train station all the way to Southern Cross.

Seriously? I don't know how long an average woman brushes her hair but I felt a quarter of an hour is a bit too much. Or maybe because I have a different perspective as a guy. I spend 20 seconds to fix my hair every morning.

Going home was a bit dramatic. Well, there was this couple on the train who were arguing about something. I couldn't hear them clearly but it looked like the lady was saying something to the guy but he was denying it. Who knows? She might be accusing the husband of cheating. Whatever it was it looked like a serious argument. I tried not to make eye contact but with the way they were going I couldn't help myself but look.

Who wouldn't?

To couples: Please don't have this kind of conversation a.k.a. arguments in public places. It's not good for kids. And adults too.

7th, Friday

The Beard

Well, there was an inexplicable phenomenon about a guy on the train this morning. He had a crazy beard. When I say crazy beard, it's one comprised of a moustache, chin, sideburns and cheeks. It was the complete package. It will probably take a week and half to shave all of it. In my exaggerated estimation it is eleven times thicker than the beard of Daniel Day-Lewis in the movie *Lincoln*. I just can't imagine how he maintains it. I wonder if he uses anti-dandruff shampoo and conditioner for his beard. This guy was wearing sunglasses as well. So it was like watching a modern Rubeus Hagrid from the *Harry Potter* movie. If you ask Thor he would probably say it is so out of this realm.

I'm curious as to whether bugs love to hang around beards.

The thicker the beard, the more bugs you attract, don't you think?

10th, Monday

No thanks!

I offered a seat to an elderly man on the train but he refused. That's okay. That's cool.

Anyway, I heard that sitting is the new smoking. Maybe that's why. I probably overreacted because it reminded me of my offer of love a long time ago that was refused. That hurt me like a paper cut.

Anyway, as with other things, any offer can be refused—offer of love (which I did), offer to buy a house (I did this too), offer to treat someone for dinner (yes, I did this as well), offer to open the door for someone (yes I still do), offer to mow someone's lawn for free (I did offer a few times but didn't take me seriously), offer to clean someone's room (I made someone to offer to me which I eventually refused anyway), offer to drink someone's coffee (I don't know about this one), and the list goes on.

To that elderly man who refused my offer, I have a message for you: _____.

11th, Tuesday

Start of my sax life

I was so excited because this morning was my first saxophone practice at the studio. I have followed *X-Factor Australia* this year and Marlisa, the grand winner for 2014, inspired me to pursue music again. I've seen her growth from being a shy schoolgirl to a superstar. It's amazing how someone can grow like that in only a short time of three or four months. She basically represents the idea that no one is too young or too old to pursue a dream. No one!

Thank you Marlisa!

I was going to document my saxophone project in a book and call it *My Sax Life*. So I went online to check if the title is available. Guess what?

It's taken. Someone already wrote a book about it with that exact title!

Anyway, if today was an entry in *My Sax Life* book, it would read like this:

On my very first day of practice, I was carrying the saxophone on my back. I got off the train station in the city and walked towards the escalator. People stared at me as if I'm carrying a big bag of guns. I just ignored them. I needed to be focused and determined.

Yes! My first day of sax. It was electrifying. I never felt this way before.

12th, Wednesday

Another day, another sax

Second day of sax life. I'm still excited. I wish I could maintain this feeling for the next twelve months. I wish someone could invent a pill or something that keeps what you're feeling or state of mind for an extended period. Or even help me use my brain to its full capacity. That would be really awesome! I wish I had that pill in the movie *Limitless*.

On the train, I stood my saxophone next to me along the aisle because I love it too much. If I didn't, there would be no leg room for me and the other passenger opposite of me. Then a guy got on the train and sat next to me. I had to squeeze in a bit more to give more room to him.

Just don't touch my sax! She's the love of my life.

13th, Thursday

PSO

This morning was the third day of my sax program. I didn't realise how heavy my saxophone actually was until today. I think my excitement in the last two days was just too much to notice the heaviness of my load. Walking up two sets of escalator at Parliament Station was not easy with a saxophone on my back. I just kept visualising myself playing the saxophone so beautifully. I squashed any thoughts of giving up.

It was very warm this morning at the studio as the air-conditioning was not working. Technology failure is often more frustrating than not having technology at all. But I'll not let that affect my saxophone practice today. No way!

I always see Protective Service Officers (PSO's) at most train stations on my way home. I actually feel more secure catching the public transport these days. It would be interesting to know what the statistics are in terms of commuting frequency rate.

Do people travel on trains more often after they deployed the PSO's at train stations?

Thank you PSO's for making us feel safe.

14th, Friday

Stop dozing off

Normally when I see people looking down, they would be looking down on their phones. This morning when I got on the train, everyone was looking down not because they were checking their phones but because they were dozing off. After a few seconds seeing all these people sleeping, I felt sleepy. I fell asleep and when I opened my eyes the train had just left Richmond station towards the city loop. I tried to pinch myself to stay awake to make sure I wouldn't miss my station.

On the train home after work, guess what? More people were dozing off. Then, I felt sleepy.

What the heck is going on here?

No dozing off tomorrow please. You are contagious! Go away!

17th, Monday

Tech stuff and boredom

Two guys were talking on the train but I couldn't hear them properly. My headphones were just too loud and I didn't want to turn them down. It looked like they were having an interesting discussion. Out of curiosity, I paused my Hillsong music and started listening to these two guys. They were talking about architecture and design. When they described about what constitutes a great design, I was able to relate to them but when they started talking about measurements, specs and technical terms, my head started to hurt. It was only 7:15 in the morning and I haven't had my caffeine dose yet. So no measurements please.

Just relax a bit, boys.

18th, Tuesday

Pen

There was an elderly man on the train who was reading with his pen sitting next to him. I didn't know if he put it there on purpose so no one will sit on it, or did he just forget? Anyways, I put my saxophone down and prepared to sit. As I was about to sit, he grabbed his pen. To be honest, whether or not he was going to pick up that pen, I was going to sit there anyway. I didn't mind staining my pants.

So if you are one of those people in the morning rush hour who put things on the seat to keep people from sitting next you, beware!

When I got off Parliament station, I was so excited for my saxophone practice that I was almost running despite the heavy saxophone on my back. I think it was because of the pen incident that made my blood flow really fast which resulted to a sudden rush of energy.

I thought if this pen incident happens every morning, I would have the energy to go to the studio every day.

19th, Wednesday

Agent Smith

A few weeks ago, I saw Agent Smith on the way to work. You know, that character in the movie *The Matrix*. Guess what? I saw him again this morning except that this time, he brought his fellow agent with him. They were sitting next to each other, wearing sunglasses and silver watches. They looked like brothers. If Neo was here in a form of an app, he could choose to be the Snapchat app so he could take both these agents with him into the matrix of oblivion. So far, both of them have been behaving well and they were not shooting Neo and everyone else. So that's good.

I sold my learner saxophone online and I brought it with me this morning to post. I would have kept it as a backup but because I live in a studio apartment where there's not much space, I had to let it go. I actually think that living in a studio apartment has a lot of benefits. I stopped buying things I didn't really need. I save money and space.

20th, Thursday

Diversion

I didn't get a seat when I got on the train so I stood all the way to the city. The train was diverted this morning to run directly to Flinders Street Station instead of going around the loop. When I got off Flinders Street Station and walked towards Collins Street, I saw a take-away-only Starbucks. I got curious. It was interesting to know how this business model would work out because people go to Starbucks not just to have coffee but also to work and meet

34

up with people. I should come back and check this place in a few months if it would still be there. If it's still going to be there, that could mean the business model is working. Perhaps, when the next train diversion happens I can come back here to check.

21st, Friday

Eyeballs

I sprinted to the train station to catch the 8:14 A.M. train and I made it. This is the latest train I needed to catch so I could still make it on time at work.

Nothing interesting happened on the train this morning. So I started to look around. I examined everyone. I needed to write something for my diary!

There was one thing I've noticed. Most people on my carriage were wearing eyeglasses. And I have a theory on this. I reckon it's because people spend more time on their smartphones and tablets these days. This includes me, by the way. That's why I'm wearing eyeglasses too. I found out from the optometrist that when you're in front of a computer, it is important to look away once a in a while to exercise your eyeballs. So don't stare on your computer for too long without taking a break. It's certainly not a healthy habit.

22ⁿᵈ, Saturday

Look after the elders

It's Saturday and I caught the tram to do some work at Hudson's Coffee on Victoria Parade. I felt relaxed doing work here and yes they have free Wi-Fi. Thank you Hudson's.

Later, I realised that I thanked them too soon because after a few minutes, they told me that were closing shortly.

Thank you very much. I didn't finish the work that I was doing. Anyway, I packed up my things and went to catch the tram to the city.

On the tram, I saw an elderly woman standing so I got up and offered my seat. I felt good. This was the second time that I offered my seat. The first one was on the tram as well on the way to Hudson's Coffee.

Let's look after our elders.

24ᵗʰ, Monday

Stop fiddling

It's Monday and guess what? My train was diverted again to run directly to Flinders Street Station.

Nice! Just what I need on a Monday morning.

I tried to go for a walk along the Yarra River but it started to rain so I started to walk the opposite direction towards Collins Street to catch the tram. My lips were hurting me. I think it's from my excessive saxophone practice the other day. I kept telling myself that this pain is just temporary and that I need to be faithful to my goal.

On my way home on the train, there was this guy on a mobile chair. I was sitting next to him and I really wanted to start a conversation but he was too busy on his iPhone. There was something in him that I was curious to know about. I was about to interrupt him when this thought came to me:

Man, he looked really occupied into what he was doing on his phone. He could be in the middle of something really important and if I interrupt him he would lose his train of thought. I better leave him alone.

And that what's I did. So I just sat there and watched him fiddle with his iPhone.

Moral lesson: There will be instances when we need to put our phones away so we can talk and connect with real people. We could be missing out on meaningful conversations. You may meet that special someone too.

Who knows?

25th, Tuesday

That was close!

I didn't have much sleep last night. Three hours to be exact. It's not good. Not good at all. I was sitting at a tram stop waiting for my tram. As the tram was approaching I stood and started walking towards it. Then, a cyclist came out of nowhere and she was pretty fast. I didn't realise how fast she was until she was four metres away from me and was about to hit me. I froze for a moment. I didn't know what to do. Now, remember that I only have three hours of sleep so I wasn't thinking properly in my capacity as a human being. Luckily, she avoided me. The tram stopped by this time. I must say though, that legally, the cyclist was supposed to stop and give way to the people boarding the tram.

Just a reminder for all our non-Melbourne drivers and even for Victorian drivers who rarely drives to the city: When the tram stops you must also stop to give way to people getting on and off the tram.

There was this girl in a somewhat unique outfit — red trench coat, red and white checker pair of pants and white pair of shoes. She was wearing a good, black-framed eyeglasses. She was carrying a polka dot bag. She was very fashionable, overall. I liked it. There was only one thing though — she was looking down her phone the whole train trip.

Coffee?

26th, Wednesday

Bono, Dumb and Dumber

I saw a guy who looked like Bono from the rock band U2. The only different was that this guy was wearing a pink outfit. He actually looked good in pink. Maybe the real Bono should try pink. I also saw Lloyd Christmas, the character played by Jim Carrey in the movie *Dumb and Dumber*. We need more of these local versions of international stars. I don't mind a local version of Barack Obama wearing Akubra, or Mark Zuckerberg wearing shorts in December. Or even Brad Pitt waiting for a tram at

Flinders Street Station. I would love to see a local version of Jennifer Lawrence with green and gold bow and arrow.

27th, Thursday

Baby face

There was this lovely couple sitting opposite of me on the train. When I looked at them more closely, I noticed a crazy tattoo on the guy's arm. He looked meek, mild and innocent. He basically had a baby face. The tattoo didn't really suit him. I wondered if it was a real tattoo and not a temporary one.

28th, Friday

The weirdest thing

Yay, it is Friday!

When I got on the train, a middle-aged woman was sitting right in the middle of a two-passenger seat. It was obvious she did not want anyone to sit next to her. This kind of behaviour increases my blood pressure sometimes. I walked towards this woman, stopped and stood next to her for couple of moments. I was curious if she was going to move to share the seat with me. She didn't move a muscle. What happened next, though, was a little puzzling.

I knew I could fit my small buttocks on one side of the seat, so I decided to sit. Just before my buttocks touched the seat, she stood up and walked away, towards the other side of the carriage.

What the heck was that about?

I thought if she didn't want to sit next to me, she wouldn't be able to smell my perfume. Her loss not mine. Not that she's the type I want to go out with. I also thought it could be racially motivated and if that was the case I wouldn't be affected either. I don't allow other people affect how I see or value myself.

DECEMBER 2014

1ˢᵗ, Monday

Mesmering eyes, disgusting phlegm

I got to the train station early to catch an early train. It's the first day of the month and a Monday.

Nice. I thought it was a good place to start something new.

I started listening to Anthony Robbins that I downloaded. He was talking about finances and the power of compounding. After that, he started talking about relationships. Normally, I would pick a book or Google a video about inspirational or motivational talks that I like or would be relevant to me. I don't think relationships and love would be relevant to me right now. I was almost going to stop listening. After a few minutes of listening into the relationships topic, I realised I stood next to a girl with very attractive eyes. I couldn't open my mouth. I was just mesmerised by her eyes.

Okay, Mr Robbins, maybe I should listen to this topic right now. Go on.

My trip home on the train was a bit disgusting. I was reading the *mX* paper when someone coughed out his phlegm and spat on the floor in front of another passenger. I could not believe what I saw!

Absolutely disgusting! I thought I was just dreaming. But nah, it was real!

Someone just spat his phlegm on the train!

2nd, Tuesday

Make-up

On my right, a guy was sitting on a priority seat with long crossed legs which means no one could sit next to him. On my left, a lady was doing her make-up from the time I got on the train until Richmond Station. That was a 15-minute trip.

How long do you need to do make-up?

Oh well, another day on the train standing next to interesting people.

3rd, Wednesday

Zombie

I didn't plan today's travel. I was indecisive about whether to drop by Starbucks to work on my blogs, or to go straight to work. I ended up going straight to the cafe near my workplace and continued reading some materials for my writing course that I'm doing through correspondence.

I didn't pay too much attention to the trains or trams today. I couldn't remember a thing when I got home. Today was one of those days where I just walked like a zombie and not have a clue about what was going on around me. Whether they bump me or I bump them I wouldn't feel a thing.

I just wanted to rest.

Zzz.

4th, Thursday

Oops, she did it again!

When I got on the train this morning, I felt a weird familiarity. When I saw this lady in her late 40s, I remember what she did in one of my previous train trips. She got up and moved away when I sat next to her.

Well, guess what?

She did it again.

What are the chances?

Unbelievable!

On the way home, there was this girl on the tram who kept staring at me. It actually made me uncomfortable. I couldn't tell if she just liked my nose.

Am I that hot or what?

5th, Friday

Don't give up!

For some reason I got up and didn't feel good although it's Friday. It took me a while to get ready before I left home this morning. I must admit that the thought of giving up and not continue this train travel book project crept my mind. I have a few projects this year and it is very easy to abandon one of them – learning the saxophone, postgraduate taxation subject or this train travel book project.

Because I started late this morning, I missed my usual express train. The next available was due in two minutes, but it stopped at all stations. I felt that it was going to take ages for me to get to the city if I caught that train. The next express was due in ten minutes. The train that stopped at all stations arrived and I was almost going to jump on. My intuition told me to wait for another eight minutes for the express one. So, I did. The next express train, which I caught, ended up getting to the city first.

8th, Monday

Discovery

When I moved to the Mont Albert, Box Hill areas, I didn't spend much time exploring the area – side streets, laneways and hidden shops. Three years on and I still keep discovering new places.

Today, for example, I discovered a free underground parking at Box Hill train station for commuters.

I used to drive to work at my previous job so I wasn't keen on getting or finding out free parking in the area.

9th, Tuesday

Into the gap

I jumped on the first carriage this morning and saw this medium size lady sitting in the middle of the seat almost occupying the whole seat. There was a little gap between her and the wall. I didn't want to tell her to move over so I sort of squeezed myself into the gap and she moved over for me. It was very kind of her.

The restaurant

I got to the train station early this morning so I caught one of the early runs. There were not many people on this train so I had the whole seat for my minus size body.

It was our work Christmas lunch today, so I was happy. When we got to the restaurant I could not believe what I saw. The place had two levels and each level had a name. We were booked on the second level but we had to enter via the first. When we entered the first level, I saw paintings of naked people. I felt weird. I don't know if it was part of the whole restaurant experience—to be greeted with those paintings. When we got to the next level, it was packed. It was a restaurant on a rooftop. The place was called Naked in the Sky. Everyone looked happy. The food was amazing though and the service was good. It had an amazing ambience. Apparently, that's what the restaurant is known for—naked paintings and good food.

After lunch I went to catch the train home from Flagstaff. When I got to the station all of a sudden I felt a little dizzy so I went to a cafe and sat there for a while. I don't know why I felt dizzy all of a sudden. It must be the paintings of naked people.

11th, Thursday

Not my day

'I don't want to remember this day. I said that I don't want to remember this day! But you have to include this in your book whether it's good or bad. No, not this one.'

This was me talking to myself. I was arguing with myself after I hit the car spot concrete marker with my low car bumper. The bumper came off and I had to quickly push it back to its place. Luckily, it was just a matter of getting the actual bumper rim locked into the brackets. By this time I could feel my blood pressure rise. Then I started to calm myself – that's just a small scratch. I love my car and for this to happen first thing in the morning is not good. Not good at all.

On the way home on the train, an elderly man got on from one of the city loop stations. I got up and offered the seat to him. He took it and just looked at me blankly without emotion. No 'thank you.' No smile, no nothing. Nice! I like this fabulous attitude.

Just nice!

12th, Friday

Sad face

I got up early to catch an early train. I had a 7 A.M. radio program. I got to the train station early but there was no express train before 6 A.M. so I had to wait for the next train which was at 6:20 A.M. So for the next twenty minutes, I was checking out other passengers at the platform.

All I saw were sad faces that said, 'Crap, it's Friday and I have to go to work!'

There was this lady in particular who was walking back and forth the platform. Looking at her frowned face, I could almost read her thoughts.

Crap, my laundry! I have to fix them tonight. I need to vacuum too. Hopefully, Dave will mow the lawn tomorrow. I need to ring him to get some milk on his way home tonight. This Carmela at work, I don't really want to hang out with her but she keeps bringing awesome cupcakes. I feel guilty. I only have four friends, I can't handle anymore.

When I got to the radio station the program was just about to start. Most of the morning crew were there and it was good to see them all. It was a full team this morning. I was glad.

On the tram on my way to work, I saw this guy's trolley full of different sorts of things. It has the sign: **Melbourne's Smallest Gallery**.

How do you tour your visitors with a trolley? I guess, you just push to wherever you want it to. Keep it going buddy.

13th, Saturday

Sweaty

I didn't check the weather last night and for some reason I assumed it was going to be cold. So I put on this thick pair of pants and a long-sleeved shirt. It turned out to be a quite warm morning. I was sweating from when I got on the train.

It's Saturday and obviously I'm not coming to work so to wear what I'm wearing on a warm day is ridiculous. People can probably smell me right now. And I didn't have my perfume with me. So I didn't worry too much about my B.O. I must say though that I did spray some deodorant before I left home this morning. That decreases the probability of a B.O. by 30% based on my experience.

I felt sticky.

I felt sweaty.

I could feel it all over my body.

15th, Monday

Graffiti on the train

I caught an early train but didn't get a seat. This was 7 A.M. Melbourne is really getting crowded. I read somewhere that in 2031, the Melbourne population is projected to reach 6 million, which means another 700,000 plus homes will be needed.

How crazy is that projection? I don't know how they calculated that but it sounds like the home builders are going to be busy. More tradesmen are needed. This means that my female friend whose name I won't mention here, will be spending more time watching these tradies work and burn some calories.

When I boarded the train. I was greeted with a massive graffiti on the wall inside the train. I didn't know what to say. Some graffiti look nice when they are done on walls but graffiti inside the train is definitely not on.

This is just not right. My day then just went downhill.

16th, Tuesday

No Standing means that

I've been thinking on the train about the Martin Place hostage drama in Sydney. I pray for the families of those two hostages who passed away. I can't even begin to imagine what those hostages have gone through. This whole Martin Place siege is all over TV, radio and newspapers. Everyone is talking about it.

I decided to do more saxophone lessons today. I wish I could play well now for those affected by the whole Martin Place siege.

After the saxophone session, I saw a black Maserati parked at a 'No Standing' zone.

'Come on man, driving a very expensive car doesn't give you permission to park there,' I thought.

17th, Wednesday

Always comes in three

Three things. Just three things.

First, I almost hit another car at the train station as I was rushing to get a car spot. Suddenly I was awake at 200%. Then I found a car spot.

Second, I only have a Zone 1 ticket today, so I had to catch the tram. It was a pain because the tram stopped at all stations. It tested my patience.

Third, the tram driver closed the door on my face. The driver could see me running towards the door. The doors were wide open while I was running. He then shut them when I was about to hop on.

Why are some tram drivers so mean? What the heck?

So I had to wait for the next one. It tested my patience again.

18th, Thursday

Three lockings

I have never taken a morning nap on a train before. I mean a proper nap – where you don't know what's happening around you. Today was the first time. I must have been really tired that I didn't have time to pick up my morning caffeine fix. Well, the nap sort of fixed me because I felt good after it. Although, it was only for about 16 minutes. It was worth skipping the coffee.

On the tram home I also had a nap. Tram takes a bit longer to get home than the train so it was hard not to nap. I don't know what's on me today. Full of napping. I'm not even pregnant.

Today was also full of locking eyes with people. Three girls to be exact.

First. When I caught a tram from Collingwood. When the tram door opened, I saw this pretty girl who I assumed was already looking at me while the tram was still moving. I could tell. I felt a little bit uncomfortable because she was still looking at me once I was inside the tram.

Someone call the cops! I don't want to get followed.

Second. On the tram home. This time the girl looked like she haven't had sleep for three days. She had big, red eyes. I tried not to look at her for too long. She might think that I like her. We only locked eyes for about a minute.

Third. There was this girl at the back of the tram who looked like a man. When she got up to get ready for the next stop, our eyes locked for about nine seconds. She definitely looked like a man but she was wearing a skirt so I assumed she was a woman. I was confused.

I think I better stop right here.

19th, Friday

Volunteers

I had a radio program this morning at 7 A.M. so I needed to get an earlier train.

I missed the train that I was supposed to catch. Luckily the next one was an express train. I felt a bit tense so I listened to some saxophone renditions of some of my favourite songs like *I Can Only Imagine* by the band called Mercy Me. I felt inspired again to continue on my saxophone learning journey. It's very easy to get distracted with a lot of things happening around – TV, YouTube, Facebook, Twitter, people's complaints you hear on the train. The list goes on.

Taking notes of what people are doing on the train, of course, is an exception. It is the 'Project.'

When I got to the radio station, it was good to see the other crew. It's amazing to work with these people who sacrificed getting up very early and coming to the station. We are all volunteers and we all want to make a difference in our community. Part of the program this morning was an interview with the Philippine Ambassador to Australia. We also interviewed the Philippine-Australia Consul based in Melbourne. The Consul's role is a volunteer capacity. I think the Consul's role is a challenging one because you're dealing with visas, citizenships, immigration, detentions, working with a student VISA, and a whole lot of other issues.

20th, Saturday

No one is here

Today is my sister's birthday. I always feel happy every year when I go to my sister's house to celebrate her birthday. Often we would celebrate her birthday and Christmas Day at the same time. It is Saturday and I do my Saturday routine – park in Carlton and catch a tram to the city.

It was weird that I was the only one on the tram. I felt lonely. There's no one to watch or listen to. There's not much for today's entry. Well, it looks like it's going to end right here. Right at this very sentence.

21st, Sunday

My body was dancing

It's the second day of the weekend. Weekend is when everything and everyone looks amazing and full of life. It's when you see sparkling eyes and attractive lips. This is when I eat Nasi Goreng with extra spice and still manage to have a big smile on my face. Unfortunately, there are only two of these days I spend every week.

Normal week is when everything and everyone seems so boring. Frowning faces, tired eyes and bigger nostrils. I spend five boring days every week for the normal week.

Sad!

I shouldn't be taking any notes about my commuting because today was supposed to be 'me' time but I felt inspired to write something.

I took advantage of the momentum that I gained in the last couple of days from my music practice. I went to do some more saxophone practice today. I enjoyed my practice today that I recorded it and uploaded on YouTube. I warn you though that it is not a very pleasant thing to listen to. I'm on my very early stage of learning so what you will probably hear may not necessarily what you would consider music.

I caught the tram towards Carlton to pick up my car and this African teenager with a loud CD player on the tram was making me dance to the beat. The music was so tempting that my body started dancing to the beats, although in my mind I didn't want to do this. I was almost like a dog wagging its owner. Luckily, he and his friends got off after a couple of stops. That's when I stopped dancing. I shall say, my body stopped dancing.

22nd, Monday

Mind over body

I was tossing and turning last night. So I got up early. It's Monday and getting to the train station as early as 6:49 A.M. was not my idea of a normal Monday. I was actually not feeling well this morning but I dragged myself out of bed.

'I can't get sick,' I was telling myself.

I have a lot of things to do today. You know the more I told myself that I am well and that I'm not going to get sick today, the more it was becoming manifested. As I got on the train, and caught my connecting tram to work, I started to feel a little bit better.

I continued saying it in my mind, 'I'm well, and I'm well, I'm well.'

By the time I got to work and turned on my computer I was starting to feel like normal. When I started working and got into the momentum, it eventually disappeared. I just drank lots of water.

Sometimes, you just need to tell off your mind.

23rd, Tuesday

Killing the Giants

I don't know if I was having a déjà vu or something. I got up early, went to the station and caught the same 6:49 A.M. train to the city that I caught yesterday.

A big guy kept looking at me that I could feel it felt like piercing my gut. It was crazy like heck. I felt like he didn't want me on the train.

I wasn't sure if it was because I looked Asian. Although I've been mistaken in the past as Indian and also Spanish. Someone even asked me if I know some places in the Cook Islands.

Anyway, I just kept reading my book *Killing the Giants* by Stephen Denny. I made sure he saw what I was reading. The book is actually a business book on how to compete in business.

24th, Wednesday

One of my favourite days

Christmas Eve is one of my favourite days of the year. The build-up of excitement in anticipation of Christmas Day is not quite the same as the Christmas Day itself. I caught the same 6:49 A.M. train to the city. Again. I actually hope that catching the early trains continues to accelerate my saxophone learning progress. It's not normally easy to get up so early in the morning. To do this for the third day in a row surprises me.

I could not wait to leave work today as I still had a couple of Christmas presents to buy. The tram from South Melbourne to Southern Cross was not as packed as I expected on a Christmas Eve.

It's Christmas break for the next four days. That means no train travels for me. No diary entries.

I'll see you guys next week.

Merry Christmas!

29th, Monday

Stare

I'm back after four days of hiatus. I enjoyed my Christmas very much and I hope you did too.

Although I missed my usual 6:49 A.M. train, I still managed to catch my usual tram to the studio to do my morning saxophone practice.

I caught the tram home and there was this elderly well-dressed lady sitting opposite me kept looking at me. It was a bit creepy. Unless you look like Brad Pitt or Natalie Portman; or lost your eyeballs this morning, you wouldn't want to be stared at by a stranger.

Instead of staring back at her, I looked out the window. Otherwise, we would have been staring at each other for the entire journey.

WARNING: To all commuters out there, staring at other passengers may cause them to feel important. Keep staring.

30th, Tuesday

Accounting systems, boring?

When I got on the train this morning, it felt dead. There were only three people on my carriage. When there are not many people on the train, you notice more details of what these few people do.

Take this girl for example, who kept looking at her mirror. There was no booger on her face. It was clean.

'Miss, you are already beautiful, no need to check in the mirror,' I was tempted to tell her but I didn't.

I didn't know why, but going past Glenferrie Station today where Swinburne University is reminded me of online accounting systems.

What the heck? Accounting systems? What do they have to do with trains and commuting?

I don't know. It could be something in my sub-conscious. I remember I wrote a blog about my prediction that accounting systems will become unnecessary and will eventually be phased out. The reason I said that was because online bank statements serve as an accounting system themselves having both credit and debit columns. Credits in bank mean money coming in and debits mean money going out. The whole idea of an accounting system is basically to organise your accounts into meaningful categories. Unless you are running a medium-sized company with a few employees, you don't need to spend much on accounting systems. Your bank statement is your accounting system as long as every expense comes out of the same bank account where all revenues are deposited, you'll be fine. GST is another story, of course.

Enough!

Boring!

31st, Wednesday

Happy New Year's Eve

What can I say, it's the last day of 2014 to catch the public transport. It's not quite the way I envisioned to finish the year with but at least reaching this far gives me a sense of accomplishment already towards this whole Melbourne travel diary project. It creates momentum. This morning on the train, I was juggling between taking notes about what passengers were doing and planning for 2015. Everyone is in the New Year's Eve mode – party mode. I was rushing to buy some books on Spencer Street to read over the break. Just when I got there, they were closing. Disappointed, I slowly walked back towards the tram stop.

While I was walking down the escalator, there was this lady talking to someone standing right next to her. I was rushing and I made sure my footsteps were loud enough for her to hear so she would give way. What happened next was interesting. I wasn't entirely sure if she heard me or not but she didn't move a muscle. I was right behind her, about four inches.

I didn't bother to say 'excuse me.'

But it just goes to show that some people are just insensitive or perhaps completely oblivious of what's happening around them. In this case, for example, I was not sure whether she was just pretending or into a really deep conversation with someone.

Anyway, that's just my little rant for today.

Happy New Year, everyone!

JANUARY 2015

2nd, Friday

Zombie

It's the first day back at work and it's a Friday.

Why am I even going to work today?

We needed some coverage today, so I had to be there. There were only three passengers on the train on my carriage. It felt absolutely dead. Like that scene in the movie *I am Legend* with Will Smith. The only difference is that there were no zombies today. Well, at least not real ones. I felt like a zombie going to the train station. This reminded me of Brad Pitt's movie *World War Z*. That was an interesting movie. It is not your typical zombie movie. The virus infection takes hold of a host in twelve seconds which is a bit unrealistic. Notwithstanding the unrealistic plot, it was a good movie. And I felt that some of the scenes in the movie were similar to what I felt this morning on the train. Everyone looked like zombies – all headed to work after a day of revelry.

There will be tram works for the whole week, so this morning I walked a few blocks from the train station to work. Nice! Just absolutely nice! I have to get a new pair of ergonomic shoes.

4th, Sunday

Free Tram Zone

I thought I'd share with you my commute today. I didn't have to as it is Sunday. I spent time with my sister and my nephews.

Yarra Trams had just introduced the 'Free Tram Zone' within the CBD so I parked my car in Parkville and caught the tram to the market. I assumed that CBD included Melbourne University in Parkville. After the market trip, we caught the tram back to Parkville. We were a stop away when I heard the tram driver announce that we have left the 'Free Tram Zone.'

'What the heck? Isn't this still part of CBD? Not that I care anyway because I have monthly pass and I'm about to get off,' I thought just when I was about to get off Victoria Market stop.

Later I found out that the 'Free Tram Zone' is within specified boundaries only within the CBD. Just because the tram stop is part of the city (within the 3000 postcode) does not make the tram stop part of the free tram zone. For example, on Swanston Street, the boundary is at RMIT stop; South Melbourne boundary would be Batman Park Stop #124 on Spencer Street. So, be careful when you go to the city and catch the tram because not always or not all tram drivers announce when where the free tram zones are.

5th, Monday

She-ra, princess of power

Monday, Monday, Monday. For the first time after a few months I thought about leaving my job. With all the time I spent commuting every single day and finishing late at work, I was seriously considering to quit. But then this book project won't be completed if I quit. The more I thought about it, the more I got serious about resigning. I had to quickly switch to thinking inspiring thoughts. Thoughts that would push me through challenges and reach my goals. One of those goals is to complete this book and to share with you all what Melbourne commuting is like.

Tram works are still in progress so I planned to walk a few blocks from work to the train station. Luckily, someone from work dropped me off at Southern Cross. I don't need ergonomic shoes now. Thank you She-ra, princess of power.

6th, Tuesday

Not a problem

A medium size girl sat next to me on the train next to me this morning. I almost didn't fit so I thought of changing seats.

That's okay. Not a problem.

I didn't change seats.

A guy with a turban and long beard staring at me. That's okay. Not a problem. Let him stare at me.

The rest of the passengers are dozing off. That's okay. Not a problem. Let them doze off. That's fine.

Sometimes observing too many people on the train makes me crazy.

7th, Wednesday

Fashionable eyeglasses make me look hotter

This lady on the train kept looking at me like she was going to eat me. I don't think I'm yummy enough!

What the heck? Am I really that hot? I'm not stopping you lady. You can look but you can't touch. Okay!

This Asian couple opposite of me are talking about something I could not understand. It sounded like they were planning to buy a car. The only thing that caught my attention was the fact that they were wearing nice looking eyeglasses. They look attractive with the eyeglasses. I guess I became more observant with people wearing eyeglasses as I got my own prescription eyeglasses recently. I reckon eyeglasses make people look attractive. That's what I reckon. What do you reckon? I reckon that you reckon that I would look hotter.

8th, Thursday

Cocoa

It's good to have your morning train trip greeted by a girl with a nose ring, carrying a heavy backpack and wearing a big cute smile. Thanks girl, whatever your name is!

Then, I got on the train and a boy politely moved to give room for me to sit next to him. Thank you to the parents who trained him. It's rare to see these values these days particularly from kids.

The tram trip was not as good as the train this morning. When I jumped on the tram on Swanston Street, it was dark. No lights nothing. It was as dark as my favourite 70% cocoa dark chocolate. I actually didn't mind it. I like working in the dark. I also like drinking coffee in dark places. So yes, I am familiar with darkness.

9th, Friday

Soaked

Today was one of my most memorable days of this whole commuting book project. I didn't want to put this as I thought it's quite embarrassing.

Stuff it, I'm willing to embarrass myself for you — the readers!

This is what happened. I got off the tram on Flinders Street. I started walking towards the Casino, not to gamble, but to cut through to Clarendon Street. After about five minutes of walking it started to trickle and I thought it was just a trickle. Then in about 7.7 seconds, it poured like crazy.

What the heck is this!

I was in the middle of my walk that I could not find any dry spot to take shelter from. I kept walking. I ran for a bit. Then I stopped and continued walking. I was soaking wet. It was like the fountain scene in the movie *Bridget Jones's Diary* like except that I didn't fall in the fountain.

You wouldn't think to bring an umbrella on a sunny day, would you?

Well, that's what I did today.

Duh!

12th, Monday

I'm angry, I'm not angry

I was standing, waiting for my train when I decided to take a seat. Once I sat on the bench, the girl who was standing next to the bench walked away.

What the heck is going on here? I did take a shower this morning. I can't be that smelly. I don't sweat that much and I didn't do jogging this morning. Come on!

Tram works were complete so my tram was back to normal today on Collins Street. Though, I wasn't happy when it didn't stop where I was waiting for it. This is what happened. I was waiting for a while at the tram stop when another tram on a different route stopped in front of me and opened its doors to let the passengers in. My tram stopped behind this other tram and also opened its doors. A number of people from the front of the tram stop ran towards my tram. I couldn't move. They jumped on and the driver closed the doors. It happened so quick that I didn't catch any of them. I could have caught the other tram and changed trams at Southern Cross.

I got angry.

I took the next tram and changed at Southern Cross. My tram was just in front of us so I ran towards the front and jumped on.

Nice! I'm not angry anymore.

13th, Tuesday

Take it easy

When I jumped on the train this morning, two blokes caught my attention. They sat very close to each other. Then they started doing some intimate things. I would like to think that they were a couple. Anyway, whether they were a couple or not, intimacy is not something you need to show in a very public place like the train. Just learn to take it easy. You'll have more time for that later on. In the meantime, just enjoy the Metro ride. Sit back and relax.

14th, Wednesday

Zero love life with orange

I was greeted with rain this morning. It reminded me of last week. I developed a phobia from last week's *Bridget Jones* scene. It's all just a memory now. Hopefully.

While I was driving to the train station, I heard on the radio that there were major delays on my train line. When I got to the station it was delayed but not as bad as they described it on the radio. Sometimes the media guys like to exaggerate things. My train was late for four minutes. I don't consider that a major delay at all.

I got on the train and saw this cute couple holding each other's hands. The guy spoke sweet nothings to the girl. I couldn't hear them. I just felt it. (Yeah, right!)

Oh how sweet!

I turned to my side only to realise that my friend Patricia wasn't there. She left me again this morning. I couldn't believe it.

Where are you, Patricia? Why did you leave me?

By the way, Patricia is my imaginary friend from university. She left me when I started eating Nasi Goreng. She said I was being racist. I didn't understand why she thought it was racist.

What?

Excuse any temporary hallucination here. I think this is what happens when you've been single for too long.

I was reading a book about viral marketing when the tram door opened on Batman Avenue. The doors opened on the right-hand side which I only realised when I was almost got squeezed like an orange. I was so engrossed with what I was reading that I ignored Batman.

15th, Thursday

No coffee fix

The train was delayed again this morning but it still went through the city loop so I was able to get off Parliament Station. Oftentimes, when the train is delayed it skips the loop and goes directly to Flinders Street.

I just made it to the tram stop when my tram to the studio arrived. It's been two weeks since I had my proper saxophone practice so I'm very glad to get back to my old morning routine again. After practice, I had to walk one block towards Victoria Parade to catch the tram from there. My saxophone was quite heavy so it was a bit of a struggle.

I was going to get coffee and drink it on the tram on the way to work.

I was half-way through the queue when I said, "Stuff this, this is too long. This barista was taking his time."

So I walked out of the cafe and caught the tram to work. No coffee this morning. That's fine.

16th, Friday

Tomato battle

I caught the 6:05 A.M. train to the city and it was not fun. I watched a lot of tomato battles on YouTube last night so I feel like going to one right now. Watching people throw tomatoes at each other can be quite entertaining. The anticipation of getting hit is worse than actually getting hit.

I had a radio program this morning so I had to catch the early train. I enjoyed the radio program this morning. We started new topics to discuss every week and it is something that listeners can look forward to every Friday morning. For this month of January, we started talking about setting up yearly goals and breaking them down into months, weeks and days. By doing it this way, you make your goals more achievable. That will build your confidence. Setting goals that are too broad makes them unrealistic. If you do, pretty soon you will abandon those unrealistic goals altogether.

I saw a $5 note and picked it up. Yes! My coffee money.

I finished late at work today. After work I rushed to the tram stop only to find out that the tram was delayed by at least half an hour. I would not even describe myself while I was waiting. I could put a dent on the tram but my self-control was as high as the Eureka tower.

18th, Sunday

Tram works again

It's Sunday and I shouldn't have taken notes about my travels.

Okay, I was waiting for the tram on Collins Street to go to South Melbourne. I've been waiting for a while and it looked like the tram was not coming. Then I realised when I looked up the notice board, that there were tram works on Collins Street. An elderly woman came up to me and asked where the trams were.

They were sent to France to pick up the goods.

Of course I didn't say that.

"It looks like they are doing some tram works up ahead," I said to her. "I might just walk to Bourke Street and catch a tram from there towards Spencer Street."

I thought she was going to follow me but she stayed there instead.

Sleep

I wanted to sleep in this morning but I just couldn't otherwise I wouldn't get a car spot at the train station. As early as 7 A.M. the car park gets full so you have to be very early and very quick.

Not sleeping in this morning meant getting a car spot. I was happy.

I felt very sleepy though so I slept on the train for 20 or so minutes. I didn't see or hear much on the train. So if a girl with a nose ring kissed a stranger on the forehead I would not have seen it. If a guy pinched my lunch from my bag I wouldn't have felt it.

I was so sleepy that I almost missed to get off the train. I then went straight to Starbucks for my caffeine fix.

What am I going do without Starbucks?

After work, I rushed to catch my tram.

The trams have been running late recently so I assumed it would be late again tonight. Based on that assumption, I thought I would get to the tram stop a little bit late and still make it.

I was wrong.

The tram was right on time.

20th, Tuesday

Yellow headphones

I caught an express train this morning. It was an old train where you have to pull the door handle to open it. Once I was seated, this guy with big yellow headphones caught my attention.

Whoa, man, why so big and yellow?

You know those people who drive flashy yellow cars. It's the same thing here with this guy with his yellow headphones. They need attention. I was his first 'attentionee' if there is such a word. If there isn't I'd be the first one to use it.

Going home, these two German-speaking girls caught my attention. I like hearing people talk in German. It's like listening to the sound of rain on my roof.

21st, Wednesday

In the face

I was running late this morning to catch the train. Luckily it was late by a minute and 43 seconds, to be exact, so I was still able to make it. I sat next to a girl and tried to smile but then she put her earphones on.

Okay, if you don't want to sit next to me, that's fine. You're welcome to change seats, if there's any available.

I'm going to the studio anyway so I'll vent all my frustration with my saxophone. Perhaps, I'm just overreacting.

I almost hit someone in the face by accident. Well, I was about to cross the street and decided to use the pedestrian lane. I quickly pressed the pedestrian button. Then I stretched my arms when this girl behind me was reaching for the pedestrian button as well. Two things – either she didn't see me press the button or she didn't care whether I pressed it or not and she wanted to press it herself as well. Based on my calculations I could have hit her in the face by accident when I was stretching before. Luckily for her, I have good peripheral vision.

22nd, Thursday

Avoid

Water came into the train and on the seat so I avoided the other half of the seat. I didn't really mind getting my pants wet. It's just water. I have zero care factor today so yes, bring some more water in.

When I got on the tram to go to the studio, this girl who was standing not far from me tried to avoid me. She tried to hide behind the side tram wall.

Do I look like a terrorist? Hmmm.

This guy standing opposite me kept looking at my saxophone bag. Every time he looked I tried to look him in the eye but then he would look away.

Do I really look like a terrorist?

After the saxophone session, I caught a tram that was so packed I almost suffocated. It was bad. Bad is actually an understatement. It was horrendous. I needed to catch a tram or I would be late for work.

23rd, Friday

Give me money

Yippee, it's Friday! Though, I was running late for my radio program this morning. So once the train doors were open I ran and climbed two sets of escalator and in less than three minutes I was out of the train station. I saw the tram which was about to turn left had just stopped at the traffic lights just a couple of metres from the actual tram stop. I tried to get the driver's attention to get him to open the door for me but he ignored me. I was so desperate to go to the studio that I knocked on the tram door. The driver didn't budge and continued to turn. I walked to the tram stop and waited for the next tram.

After radio, I rushed to catch my tram when this homeless guy asked me for some money. I didn't have any cash with me so I apologised to him. Sometimes I question the integrity of these people asking for money on the streets whether they're genuine or not. The reason I say this is because I was a victim of a scam. One night while I was walking on Swanston Street a guy stopped me and asked for money. He said he needed money for his bus fare so he could go back home to Sydney. He looked very sincere so I gave him some money. I was glad that I was able to help someone.

However, an interesting thing happened a few weeks after that night. I was walking towards Starbucks to do some work when a guy stopped me to ask for some money to buy for his bus fare to Sydney. To my surprise, it was the same guy a few weeks ago who asked me for money. He obviously didn't remember me but I remembered him. He used the same script. At that moment, I realised I was a victim of a scam.

He should have come up with a different script.

24th, Saturday

Long Australia Day weekend

Today is a very short one. It's Saturday and it's the long Australia Day weekend. And I have to spend some time with my family. I caught a tram from Carlton to the city to get some lunch. This Asian lady who looked like a tourist asked for some directions from the tram driver. As I was sitting in the middle of the tram, I didn't hear the name of the place she was asking for but the driver didn't know where it was. I could see the disappointment in the lady's face. I would assume most tram drivers would know Melbourne.

Do you think tram drivers know or should know major places in Melbourne? Anyway, I will enjoy my long Australia Day weekend.

27th, Tuesday

Military operation

12 o'clock: I took a nap on the train. When I opened my eyes a well-dressed man was looking at me. I didn't know exactly if it was a guy or a guy pretender.

3 o'clock: A guy was taking a nap too.

8 o'clock: There was a cute girl. It was a bit hard to see from where I was but when someone's cute, it's not hard.

On the train home, a very interesting thing happened. A phone started to ring. Ten seconds later, it still kept ringing. Twenty seconds, and it was still ringing. That phone kept ringing like crazy for a couple of minutes. Everyone was looking at everyone.

Then, an elderly man finally asked, "Whose phone is that?"

That's when the phone stopped ringing. No one responded to his question. No one knew whose phone was ringing. It sounded like it was coming from a bag and there were quite a few people with bags on our carriage.

28th, Wednesday

Never underestimate an elderly

I got off the train at Parliament Station and was about to step on the escalator when an elderly woman came from behind and overtook me. She started walking up the escalator. So I was just behind her and tried to make my pace a little bit faster. After a few seconds I noticed that she was quite a few steps ahead of me. She walked pretty fast and I could not keep up. Mind you I was carrying a laptop with me. I'm not making excuses. Okay, I concede. The woman was a lot quicker than me. She probably goes to the gym. Who knows? Maybe I should up my game and do more jogging regularly.

The fast elderly woman inspired me, that on the way home, I overtook two people talking on the escalator. I was walking down the escalator quite fast. I could see them talking so I made sure that they could hear my footsteps to give them enough warning that I was in a hurry to catch my train.

Guess, what?

They ignored me.

I could see a gap on the right-hand side so I squeezed myself in. I was just in a hurry to catch my train and was quite annoyed that they didn't move. Perhaps, I can attribute this to the elderly woman who inspired me this morning.

29th, Thursday

000

I sat next to a lady who was trying to read my travel notes. So I tilted my phone a little bit. Then she looked me in the eye.

'What the heck now?' I thought.

Then I looked away.

Sometimes I take extra care when writing my travel notes on the train. Other passengers do read the text message you're typing, the email you're trying to edit and of course the travel notes you're scribbling.

Going home on the tram this guy was wearing a shirt with profanity and drugs. He had bloodshot eyes. Scariest eyes I've ever seen. I tried to avoid him. Sometimes I get paranoid that I type 000 on my phone so it's ready just in case anything happens.

30th, Friday

Public transport vs driving

I had a radio program this morning and it was really good. I enjoyed our panel discussion. It was worth getting up early and catching the 6:05 A.M. train even though I was half asleep. We discussed about the pros and cons of catching the public transport compared to driving. In my case for example, I find more benefits in catching the public transport. First of all, I'm writing this book about my daily train travels. So I have to catch the train. Other benefits are:

- Productive use of time (reading a book, study, etc.)
- Savings in petrol, parking and mileage

However, it has disadvantages:

- other passengers sneezing or coughing and not covering their mouth
- weird and scary people on the train
- packed trains in peak hours
- cancelled or delayed trains

Like this morning for example on the train. I was planning my 2015 when this double plus size guy opposite of me kept staring at my face.

What's with the stare man? It's freaking me out.

Casual look or glimpse is fine but to stare at someone for ten minutes is absolutely not normal.

Sometimes the stress of catching the public train and driving to work are comparable but it all depends on you and your circumstances. If you value savings and not having to worry about parking in the city then you will probably catch the train. If you value having your own seat, listening to you own car stereo and not having to worry about 'weirdos' you'll probably prefer driving.

THIS CHAPTER IS DEDICATED TO THE SPANISH GAL AT PARLIAMENT

FEBRUARY

1ˢᵗ, Sunday

Heartbeat

I thought I'd start my February 'tramelogue' (tram + travelogue) on a Sunday. So I did. I went to the city and saw the brand new tram on Bourke Street. I heard that it was built in Melbourne. I was excited to have my first ride. So I patiently waited for the next one.

I got on the brand new tram towards Spencer Street and these two guys with bloodshot eyes at the back of the tram, looked at me or shall I say stared at me. You know, the sort of look that makes your heart beat faster. I normally like to sit at the back but when I saw them, I turned and walked the opposite direction. I sat on one of the front seats instead. I sat around people with normal eyes.

Then my heart started to beat normally.

2ⁿᵈ, Monday

Right on time, peace and prosperity

The 7:03 A.M. train arrived at 7:02:20 to be exact. It allowed 40 seconds for passengers to get on. That's Melbourne train for you today. Amazingly right on time! I don't know if it's going to be the same tomorrow. Well, punctuality rate of Melbourne trains is at 93% last month so there is a good chance it will be on time tomorrow. When things are on time, you can plan things and accomplish them as scheduled. I wish everything is on time.

I heard someone speak today about 'Peace and Prosperity.' That stuck in my mind and heart. I suddenly felt a strong feeling to start applying those concepts. I actually thought about starting a website called *peaceandprosperity.com.au* but when I went home to look it up I found out that it was already taken. I had a feeling that it wouldn't be available so I wasn't overly disappointed.

That's okay. Let's leave the owner of that site in peace and prosperity.

3rd, Tuesday

Insensitive, rude, sweet, tough and gibberish

The train was late this morning by about two minutes. I didn't cry so that's good. Two minutes is only half of a *Matchbox Twenty* song.

When I got on the train, this guy in his 50s was sitting in the middle of a two-seater priority seat. No one else could sit next to him. This was morning peak hour folks. For someone to have the whole seat to himself is not on. Definitely not!

When I looked over the other carriage through the glass door, I could see a woman typing on her phone. She was sitting in the middle of a two-passenger seat as well.

I've seen a lot of these types of passengers on the train lately. They want the whole seat for themselves although they can see that there are a lot of passengers standing around them. From what I've seen in the last few months of my daily commute, more passengers are becoming insensitive to other passengers. The ones that are kind enough to offer seats to people with special needs are the very ones who have special needs. The ones that you would expect the least – children, elderly and mothers.

On the train home, a cute Asian girl moved to give me more room to sit next to her. There was already enough room for my small bottom but when she saw me carrying a heavy bag, she moved a little bit further. Thank you! We need more passengers like you.

When I got off the train, I saw an elderly couple holding hands on the escalator. It was quite inspiring to watch. Romantic! I don't see much of those these days. When I was about to get on the escalator a medium size girl overtook me and walked up really fast on the right-hand side of the escalator. She was faster than me. I was completely taken by surprise.

On the train home, I saw a girl with a tattoo on her leg. She was travelling with a big, hard-muscled guy, who I assumed was her boyfriend. A tough guy, I'd say. I was looking at her tattoo because it had quite an interesting design. It looked like a dragon with a hat that has massive wings. Anyway, I had to stop looking lest being told off by her tough boyfriend. I had these scenes in my mind:

Hey, you! Small man! What are you looking at my girlfriend's leg?

No, I was looking at the tattoo, not the leg!

What do you mean?

You heard me, sir! Tattoo, no leg! By the way, I'm Dwayne Johnson's second cousin from a lost generation. You better not mess with me. I have his number on my phone. He'll beat you up if you touch me.

Get lost! And stop looking at my girlfriend!

I already told you. No leg, only tattoo!

A few minutes before my station, two men got on the train and started walking back and forth on my carriage and the next. I didn't know if they were looking for a very nice train seat without stains or dirt or what but I was raising my eyebrows. They were talking gibberish. I tried to make sense of what they were talking about but eventually gave up.

'What the heck are these guys doing?' I thought.

I couldn't wait to get off. I could see them at the corner of my eye. By the way, enhanced peripheral vision is a skill I have developed during my train and tram travels.

4th, Wednesday

Don't forget to top up your myki card

I didn't realise that my myki card has run out of credit. I'll give you a brief information about myki. I normally buy a 28-day myki pass which gives me daily access to public transport, train, tram and bus for four weeks. This is different from myki money which is what occasional commuters use. So if you normally drive to work and occasionally catch the public transport, myki money would be a better option. My 28-day pass is now cheaper than last year because this year I can purchase a ticket for Zones 1 and 2 for the price of Zone 1. I also have some myki money credit in case I run out of myki pass credit. So once the myki pass is finished, myki money will apply, until you top up your myki pass.

I went and tapped my myki card onto the myki card reader but it said 'Declined.' I tapped it again and it still said 'Declined.' I have both myki pass and myki money. It should use one of those at least. I stood there at the scanner causing delay to other passengers behind me. I ran to the Metro counter and had the staff check my myki card. Apparently, my card ran out of both myki pass and myki money. I then realised that in the last couple of days I've been using my myki money because my myki pass has ran out few days ago.

I caught the next express train because of the delay in topping up my myki card. I normally good at planning things like this. Obviously, not today. Oh well, I'm human. I make mistakes.

When I got off the Parliament Station, a girl in her gym outfit was walking quite fast behind me and I could feel the pressure for me to walk faster. I thought I was the fastest escalator walker in Melbourne.

Not today Renelo, not today!

So I walked as fast as I could. That was probably the fastest walk I had at a train station.

On my way home, I dropped by Krispy Kreme to buy some donuts.

Yum!

That meant missing my usual scheduled train and catching the next one.

5th, Thursday

The Good, the Bad and the Ugly

I think I saw Clint Eastwood on the train this morning. He was wearing his usual sunglasses. He didn't bring his gun though. He was just sitting there like a _____.

Jokes!

My brother watches Clint Eastwood movies so I get to watch them every time I go to his house. These are old action movies set in the 70's. I noticed with old movies, the characters moved faster than the modern action movies. They drew their guns in a blink of an eye, literally.

For example, in the movie, *The Good, The Bad and The Ugly*, there was this famous Mexican standoff. It was a confrontation of three men armed with guns. That standoff scene in that movie was almost six minutes. Imagine, three guys looking at each other for six minutes waiting for the first one to draw a gun. Well, on the train this morning, it felt like a Mexican standoff scene – the guy who looked like Clint Eastwood, myself and the train driver, minus the guns.

I was more intrigued with the couple next to me. An Asian girl with a tall Caucasian guy. I actually liked looking at them as a couple. I felt like they were meant for each other.

I hear some people say you should try to be with someone from your own culture so you don't have much conflict or differences in your ways of doing things, customs, etc. I disagree. That is a very limited view of living life. Sure there are benefits of being with someone who shares the same culture or heritage but I think being with someone from a different culture or heritage creates curiosity to learn more about the other person. However, this requires an open mindset. You need to be willing to learn and discover new things and acknowledge that some of those things in the form of customs and traditions of the other person, may sometimes surprise or even shock you. In the end, it requires humility and lots of patience. Besides, love knows no boundaries. If you love the person, you can learn everything about her or him.

Speaking about boundaries, I enrolled myself to a tax law subject at a university. That's to add to the list of things I don't even know how I would be able to accomplish. My full-time job, this book project, my business on the weekends, learning the saxophone, playing drums twice a month. I don't think I can add a girlfriend project on my list.

Please, no!

Anyway, I went to pick up my reading materials before I started work. It was only about five inches thick. On the tram to university, two students right at the very back of the tram got squeezed by the tram door when they tried to get off at the RMIT stop. They were alive. The driver must not have seen them in his side mirror. If I were one of those guys, I would be very angry. To tram drivers, please look after your passengers. Please don't squeeze them.

On the tram to work, I noticed two tourists who were speaking in Spanish. They were holding their luggage and I heard a few swear words in their conversation. I know a little bit of Spanish. At least I knew they were not swearing at me.

On the train home I sat next to a girl reading a law book. It wasn't tax law. It was criminal law. It was easy to read her book from where I was sitting so I started reading a couple of paragraphs. It was an interesting read. Hopefully, she didn't mind. She seemed like a nice girl anyway.

6th, Friday

Amazing sax this morning

I caught the 6:05 A.M. train again. Once I sat, this girl opposite me started to do some stretching towards my leg room. I was shaking my head. I didn't know if she was trying to send a message or what. I think that message was whether or not she wanted to swap socks because my socks are longer and I could see her short rainbow socks sticking out. I didn't mind swapping. I actually like rainbow socks.

I did some saxophone practice this morning before going to work. I was in the mood to practice so I stayed a little bit longer than usual at the studio. After the sax session, I had to run as fast as I could to catch my tram. Blame it on the amazing sax this morning.

I was typing discreetly on my phone about my amazing sax this morning. I had to tilt my phone a little or the guy next to me would see it. I was conscious that he would misread it as 'amazing sex this morning.'

8th, Sunday

Sunday swim

I caught a tram to South Melbourne this morning. On the way home I had to wait long for the tram to come. I was thinking there could have been an accident. Or maybe I was just being impatient.

I thought I should wait for a bit more. I already waited that long. I might as well wait for another forever.

When the tram arrived, it was packed. As in, jam-packed! My dilemma was whether to get on the tram or not. If I jump on, it would be very hard for me to move. My ability to breathe would also be impaired. If I don't take this tram, I could be waiting for another 30 minutes or even more.

So when the doors opened, I took a deep breath like you do when you go swimming. Then I jumped on board. I managed to squeeze my minus-size body on the tram. I must admit it was quite smelly and muggy. Just imagine everyone's odour combined in one circuitous flow inhaled by everyone. There's nothing like it.

9th, Monday

Just do it!

This girl on the train occupied the whole seat with a big bag sitting next to her. I looked closely and it was a big bag of clothes. The girl and the big bag on the train. I stood next to her trying to send a message that I would like to sit down. I don't think she got the message. She didn't move at all.

I have strong legs. I eat vegetables and red meat. So yes, I'm fine thank you.

My tram home was very late. We're talking half an hour delays. I wasn't angry. I was furious like the *Nando's Triple X Hot Sauce*. I could feel smoke coming out of my ears. I got on the tram and for some reason I regained my composure after being dipped into the *Nando's Hot Sauce*.

I heard this guy talking to his mate about his idea of writing a book, compiling all a hundred interviews that he'll be conducting.

I thought to myself, 'Just do it man!'

So hopefully he pursued that idea. I hear a lot of people talk about good ideas but don't do anything about them.

10th, Tuesday

Cute Ugly Betty

When I got on the train at Box Hill, I saw 'Ugly Betty' from the American TV comedy series, except that this one is cuter. I don't even know why they call her 'Ugly Betty' when she's actually cute. Well, to me at least. I must admit the more I catch the trains and tram, the more I see celebrity look-alikes. I like it. I don't need to go to Hollywood.

I didn't make it to the express train so I had to catch the next one but it stopped at all stations. Most of the seats were taken so I decided to stand. Shortly thereafter, an elderly man got on the train. He couldn't find a seat so he stood not very far from where I was standing. Everyone was either dozing off or looking down. No one noticed or bothered to offer this man a seat.

Do people care for the elderly anymore?

Anyway, I did a lot of deep thinking this morning for some reason. When I got to the city I was running to catch my tram to South Melbourne. The driver closed the tram doors in my face. I don't know what to do with some of these drivers sometimes. They leave the door open while you're running towards it. Then they close the door in your face.

That's just nice.

11th, Wednesday

The Orange Man

I think I saw the sweetest thing on the train this morning: A man wiping his lady's shoes. However, I noticed that while he was doing it, his face was looked very serious. His lady (I assumed that was his lady) never smiled or said anything to him. She kept looking straight. I was sitting there wondering whether they were actually a couple or not. It's just weird to see someone do a kind and sweet thing to someone without some kind of reaction. Not even a 'thank you'.

After a few minutes I saw the same lady started talking to the guy. Then I By the way, they talked to each other I realised they were a couple. Though, still no smile from the lady. Luckily, they didn't see me watching them the whole time. I was a few metres away and in a strategic position. All good.

Opposite me was an older guy with what looked like office files. He had a whole stack of manila folders next to him on the train. He was busy writing notes on one of the files. This guy doesn't stop working. Not even a train commute can stop him. Hopefully, he doesn't bring those folders in the toilet, with him.

On the train home, this guy was making me feel uncomfortable. He was wearing an orange shirt, orange pair of pants like a prisoner. I don't know if he was wearing an orange underwear. I didn't ask him. I had a feeling he was.

12th, Thursday

Woman's Day

I got to the train station at 7:04 A.M. past my scheduled 7:03 A.M. train. Thinking that I missed my train, I got out of the car and started walking slowly. A lot slower than usual. When I got to the platform, I found out that the 7:03 A.M. train was delayed by five minutes and didn't get to the platform just after 7:08 A.M. I have just missed it by ten seconds. I started blaming myself for walking slower this morning.

On the train, I was surrounded by old ladies. One of them was reading the *Woman's Day* magazine. I was standing behind her while she sat on the priority seat. I could clearly read it from where I was standing so I started reading as well. She saw what I was doing so she turned around and gave me a nasty look.

Okay, fine. Lady!

So I looked up the ceiling for about seven seconds. Then I read her magazine again when she wasn't looking. After a couple of minutes, she looked at me again with the same nasty look. This time I tried to look away towards the window. I was tempted to read her magazine again for the third attempt but decided not to.

13th, Friday

Fifty dollars

I caught the 6:20 A.M. train to the city. I initially read it as 6:26 A.M. which didn't make sense because there is no 6:26 A.M. train at my station. I jumped on the train and it wasn't quite the way I expected because there were already a lot of passengers that early.

What were they thinking?

Most of them were tradesmen. I sat next to one of them. He was sleeping. Suddenly, I felt sleepy too.

'Stop. Renelo, wake up!'

When the train was approaching Richmond Station, the driver announced that the train would run direct to Flinders Street instead of going around the city loop. It added a few minutes to my travel time because I had to catch a connecting tram to the studio for my radio program this morning.

The tram was due to arrive in seven minutes. After seven long minutes of standing, there was no sign of any tram coming. Then, I looked as far as I could at both directions and there was definitely no sign of a tram. I was tempted to just walk to the studio which would take me around 20 minutes. So I started walking towards the studio, hesitantly. About halfway through, I could hear the tram approaching behind me so I ran across the street towards the tram stop. I was still half asleep but was awaken by the car's loud horn. I was so excited to hear the tram that I didn't bother checking the road for cars. I almost got run over. The lady driver looked me in the eye.

The heck lady, watch the road. Can't you see I'm crossing!

I gave her a _____ then I jumped on the tram.

I jumped off the tram and rushed towards the studio. On the way, I thought I saw a $50 note on the footpath, just outside an old house. I didn't know what I was thinking but I ignored it. Perhaps I was just imagining things. Maybe I was just rushing that I wasn't thinking straight. I also thought it can't be a real $50 note. Maybe someone put it there and tried to record people's reaction on camera. I didn't want to be on that TV show, What Would You Do (WWYD).

To those who may not know about the show, What Would You Do (WWYD) is an American hidden camera TV program where actors act out scenes of conflict or controversy to see how people would react.

Once I was at the radio station I kept thinking about the $50 note. I started to blame myself.

Why the heck didn't I pick the $50?

After the program I walked to the tram stop past the spot where that $50 was sitting and of course it wasn't there anymore. In hindsight, I realised I should have picked up that $50 note. I was literally pinching myself because of what I did or shall I say didn't do. I tried to comfort myself and prayed that whoever picked up that $50 probably needed that money more than I do.

There was a bit of a drama on the train on my way home. While I was listening to my headphones, a family of four: mom and dad and their two children were laughing out loud (lol). It was good to see one happy family. While the train was slowing down for the next stop, the couple got up and the children followed. Then the train stopped. Mom and dad got off the train first and the two children behind them were walking when the train doors closed. I was standing close to the door so when I saw that the children were left behind I jumped towards the door button to open it. It didn't open. I pressed it really hard a few more times. It still didn't open. Then the train started to move and the children started crying. They were laughing just a few minutes ago and now they're crying. By this time, other passengers also got up and pounded the door and the wall trying to get the driver's attention. Then a lady found the intercom button and spoke to the train driver about what happened. At the next stop, two Protective Service Officers were already waiting for the kids.

Phew!

16th, Monday

Broken sentences

When I got on the train, I saw a familiar pretty face. I couldn't remember how or when but I was confident I met this girl before. I was going to go up to her and say hello but for the life of me I couldn't recall anything about her.

Crap, shall I or shall I not? What if she ignores me?

I couldn't open my mouth. I stood there frozen.

I got off the train pinching myself for my inability to unfreeze.

Then I caught my tram. It was packed and it looked like I couldn't fit my body in. I thought I'd just wait for the next tram. I changed my mind in the last minute and jumped on the tram and squeezed myself in. I did fit my small body in.

On the train home, this lady was talking loudly on the phone with someone. I had my headphones on but I could still hear her. I only heard broken sentences and some of them didn't make sense as I was listening to my music. Some of them were:

"Leaves might die before we eat them."
"If you put in the cage rather than container it might fall out."
"Most people are boring. Very rarely I get my clothes altered.
"I need to call a person first."

17th, Tuesday

No hot water no shower

I got out of bed, did some stretches and jumped in the shower. I turned the tap on and almost screamed. No hot water! The hot water system must have been broken overnight. I froze in the shower for fifteen seconds. I felt sticky.

Crap! I couldn't really call in to say I wasn't coming because I didn't have a shower.

So I prepared to leave home anyway to go to the train station. I heard on the radio that a lady was fatally hit by a truck on Collins Street and that trams were diverted out of Collins Street to La Trobe Street. This made me sad and my shower issue became insignificant.

I went to the studio to do some sax. After the sax session I went to catch the tram which was delayed because of the accident this morning. I kept thinking about that lady who was hit by a truck. It reminded me that life is too short and we should really try to be happy every day and not worry about things. We should be kind to people. We should love them.

Okay, I need tissues.

On the train home. I decided to stand even though there were plenty of empty seats. I've been sitting all day at work. I leaned on the back of the priority seat. Then a couple got on at Richmond Station and sat on the priority seats I was leaning against. The girl sat on the guy's lap and they started kissing. This went on for minutes and they kept touching my back.

'Don't involve me in your kissing there people! You can kiss but please don't touch my back!' I was yelling in my mind.

18th, Wednesday

Such is life

I waiting for the 7:17 A.M. train as I assumed the 7:14 was already gone. It was showing on the screen that the 7:17 was due to arrive. Then a train arrived just seconds after 7:14. Then someone announced that it was the 7:14 am train.

What the heck is happening here?

I quickly jumped in. When I got on the train, a teenager sitting next to a massive bag of clothes. She had her crutches on the priority seat. Her bandaged right foot was resting on the bag while she was reading a book.

I saw an awkward moment while I was waiting for my tram. A guy gave a big smile to a girl who was about to hop on the tram. There was no reaction on the girl's face. She completely ignored him. The reaction on the guy's face was not so good either. It looked like he was hurt inside.

That's alright mate, I've been there. It hurt but it will pass.

On the way home I saw a girl reading *True History of the Kelly Gang*. I don't want to talk about Ned Kelly or whether he was a hero or an outlaw. Regardless of what or who you consider him to be, his story impacted many people in one way or another.

As his famous last words said, 'Such is life.'

19th, Thursday

Stalker or not?

What are the chances of catching a train with the same guy, on the same carriage of the same train, every morning for four consecutive days? Well, that is what happened to me this week.

Is he stalking me? I'm definitely not stalking him.

With this next thing I saw, I didn't know whether to feel sorry or laugh. This schoolboy was sleeping while hugging the pole. It was smart of him to do that so he won't fall when the train breaks or stops.

On the tram on my way home, a guy was standing right next to the right-hand side door. We drive on the right-hand side in Australia so the right-hand side tram doors are not used except at certain stops. Batman Park is one of those stops. Tram doors open at the right-hand side at this stop instead of the normal left-hand side doors. While we were approaching Batman Park stop, this guy was completely oblivious that it's going to open on the right-hand side and unless he moves he will get slammed by the door. I had two options. First, I don't let him know so I could watch him get smashed by the door. Second, remind him that the doors will be opening on the right-hand side and save him from getting squeezed.

I did option number two.

20th Friday

Hepatitis A

I didn't get a chance to make my breakfast at home so I dropped by McDonald's this morning at their take-away booth but no one was there.

Stuff it! I'm just going to have Weight Watchers' Macadamia and Cranberry. I have the whole pack in my drawer at work.

When I got on the train this guy who was sitting on the priority seat was busy on his iPad. He occupied the whole seat. Another one of those people who don't want anyone sitting next to them. I stood next to him and he still didn't move. He kept reading his iPad. When I got off the train I saw a couple. Well, I assumed they were a couple. The guy was in his late 40s and the girl looked like she was 18. They were holding hands. At first I never really thought they were a couple because of the age difference. I wanted to think they were father and daughter.

I almost stared at them but when they saw me looking at them, they held their hands even tighter.

Okay, they were a couple.

I had the radio program this morning so that was fun. We talked about Hepatitis. There has been a lot of talk about Hepatitis and frozen berries in the social media so we interviewed a doctor to enlighten us. I don't want to elaborate about it but it is basically an infection of the liver. There are a few symptoms like nausea, fever, diarrhoea and jaundice which is the yellowing of the skin. It is a contagious disease and it can be spread by poor sanitation. It can also be transferred by the food that we eat. It was an interesting discussion.

On the train on the way home, this very tall girl got on the train and I was standing next to her. It made me look really short. I'm already short and she just made me shorter.

What the heck?

23rd, Monday

In your dreams!

I didn't hear the alarm this morning so I got up late. I must have been in a really deep sleep. As much as I wanted to blame myself, I didn't want to complain for having slept. I have insomnia, so to have a good, deep sleep is something that I really value.

On the train this morning, I overheard two schoolgirls talking about their siblings. One of them was saying how she and her sister share a blanket. When they go to bed, it's all fine, but in the middle of the night when it's cold, her sister would pull the blanket more towards her and this girl would wake up the next day freezing with no blanket on her.

In front of me were two schoolboys reading while standing. It's funny to see the juxtaposition: two girls talking and two boys reading.

Another girl in red I could see a few metres from where I was sitting. She looked like she was in her 20s but she got up and walked towards the door next to me I started to realise she was in her late 40s. I definitely need to bring my eyeglasses next time. When she started walking I thought for a second that she was going up to me and maybe say hello or get my number.

24th, Tuesday

Nose ring, badminton, squeaking

I caught the train this morning and sat next to a girl with a nose ring. It actually looked good on her. There are people who look really good with nose rings and there are those who look like _____.

On the tram home, there was a badminton sports bag on the floor. It looked like it was abandoned.

Is this a bomb or something? What the heck am I going to do? Maybe, someone must have forgotten it.

My thoughts were running crazy. Then a guy got up from a few metres and grabbed the bag. I assumed it was his, so I had a sigh of relief.

No bomb!

25th, Wednesday

LYNX

I wanted to catch the 7:03 A.M. train. I went to the train station early. I parked and then sprinted to the platform. I made it! I was sweating on the train and the warm morning made me worse.

Luckily I sprayed LYNX deodorant this morning so I thought, 'I'm safe. I'm not going to smell.'

I was walking really fast as I wanted to get out of Parliament Station as soon as possible so I could work on my website. However, a woman stopped me to help her get the bottle of water stuck in the vending machine. She already paid for it and was pounding the vending machine to get the bottle of water out. We tried to pound the machine again but nothing was happening. I had a quick look inside and the machine looked like it was faulty. I told her she needed to ring the 1300 number on the vending machine.

After I work, I went to Bourke Street to get a haircut. I paid $10. Amazing value. Then, I caught the train home from Melbourne Central. While I was waiting for the train, I saw a couple kissing. It was a pretty intense, passionate kissing. I tried not to watch them. Then I looked away.

26th, Thursday

Selfie

I couldn't stand what I was watching this morning on the train. A girl was taking selfies at least fifty times. It felt like I was watching a movie called *Selfie, selfie, and selfie.* Okay, maybe I'm exaggerating. Anyway, there is no such movie. Even if there is it would be very painful to watch. Imagine if it's your full-time job to take selfies. Eight hours a day, with an hour lunch break.

Anyway, it was funny to see this girl making fifty different faces. She didn't care who was watching around her obviously.

On the train home, two teenagers sat on the floor when there were a few empty seats available. I had no idea why. It's probably because the floor is _____.

27th, Friday

Making faces

This girl on the train on the way to Richmond Station was reading her iPhone while making faces. She would smile, then frown and then smile again. She then started typing on her phone.

While I was walking down the escalator, about halfway through, I stopped. A big guy had both of his big and muscled arms stretched, rested on both hand rails. Then he noticed me and took his arms off the rail so I could go through. Tough but good guy. Thanks boss!

At the platform, this girl with her push bike was also waiting for the train. She then pulled her sleeves up a bit. Then I noticed her crazy tattoo on her arm. It looked like a sword and a dragon. I saw similar tattoos but on tough big guys. I didn't think that she would have that sort of tattoo because she had a meek and mild face.

MARCH

1ˢᵗ, Sunday

Awkward Sunday

Summer is finally over and it is officially autumn. I caught the tram to South Melbourne.

On the tram to South Melbourne, I locked eyes with a girl for a few seconds. Then I looked away. After a few seconds I looked in her direction and we locked eyes again for a few seconds again. It felt awkward, so I looked away again.

I was telling myself, 'Renelo don't look in her direction. Don't you dare!'

Guess what?

I couldn't help myself. I looked in her direction for the third time and we locked eyes again. This time, it was little bit longer than the first two. I didn't know what to do. I froze for a moment while our eyes locked. Then the tram turned left and some of the passengers who were standing moved between the two of us. I couldn't see her anymore. After a couple of stops some of the passengers got off. I tried to check if the girl was still there but I couldn't find her.

I lost her.

2nd, Monday

Miserable Monday

When I got on the train this morning, all of a sudden a feeling of sadness came upon me. I didn't know why. Then I looked around and all I saw were people looking miserable. I know why—it's early Monday morning and they are back to work again after a long weekend.

It was the same scenario on the tram—all were miserable. One lady in particular, she looked so miserable that she looked like she has aged eleven years extra that morning. The misery from the passengers was so contagious that I started to also feel miserable before I even started work.

I don't want it. Go away!

3rd, Tuesday

Nothing's Gonna Change My Love for You

I've been listening to a saxophone player that I discovered on YouTube. Her name is Kaori Kobayashi. She is from Japan. I probably played her video of *Nothing's Gonna Change my Love for You* a hundred times. That inspired me to keep going with my saxophone lessons. So this morning I carried my saxophone with a renewed vigour, fresh mind and enduring love for sax.

What the heck? That means I'll be doing more practice at the studio.

The saxophone is normally heavy but this morning it felt light on my back. Thank you Kaori.

Today is our day Kaori. Just you, me and the saxophone.

4th, Wednesday

Oatmeal

I was standing on the train to the city when a guy pulls out his lunchbox from his bag.

'He's not going to eat his lunch, is he?' I thought.

Then he opened the lunchbox, grabbed a spoon and he started eating. Then I realised it was oatmeal. The guy was eating his oatmeal breakfast on the train. I don't know what is happening to our world today.

What's next? Someone cooking bacon and eggs on the train? Maybe someone making a peanut butter toast.

5th, Thursday

Fart

It was a very early start for me today. I had to get up at 5 A.M. to prepare for a breakfast client meeting in the. I had stomach pains when I got up this morning. I think I put too much chilli on my food last night. I felt a lot of gas in my stomach this morning. I accidentally released some gas from my stomach at the train station while waiting for the train on the platform. The people around me of course started to look around wondering where the smell was coming from. There are about seven people close-by. It was beyond my control. I was actually doing them a favour because the smell itself was enough to wake them up.

Today is the first day of semester. So after work, I caught the tram to university for my 6:00 P.M. tax class. There was a pretty bad smell on the tram and I tried to figure out where it was coming from but the tram was too packed. It was much like the people at the platform this morning who were curious to find out who farted.

6th, Friday

Wake up!

On the train to Richmond this morning, these three ladies were talking about a guy who gets paid too much for doing nothing. By the way they talk, they sounded like they were teachers. I was not overly impressed by the way they talk about other people.

On the tram to work this bearded guy with sunglasses looked weird. His beard seemed fake. I was curious to know whether it was real or not so I walked towards him. When I was about seven inches from him, I even looked closer. That's when I could confirm that it was real!

While I was looking at this guy's beard, the restaurant girl that I buy my lunch from was also on the tram. She tried to smile at me but I was too busy checking out this guy's beard so I didn't notice her at first. She looked away. That's when it occurred to be that it was the girl who serves us lunch at a Malaysian restaurant near work. I tried to smile back at her and when she looked in my direction she smiled back. I don't normally get a smile back from girls so I was glad that she did.

7th, Saturday

Know how to get around places

While I was walking towards Bourke Street to catch the tram, I noticed quite a lot of people at the tram stop and wondered what was happening. I was in a rush to go to the studio for my saxophone sessions so whatever what was happening at the tram stop could not stop me from getting to the studio. When I looked at the overhead electronic notice board, I could see the tram disruption notices but people were still waiting for the trams.

I was already late for my studio sessions so I had to look for other options. I ran to the next street, Collins Street, to see if I could catch a tram from there instead. While I was running I realised I had to check if Collins Street trams were also affected or not. I just assumed they were operational. Anyway, I was right. So I jumped on straight away.

It's good to know your city. It pays if you know how to get around places. It can save you time.

10th, Tuesday

Long service

I didn't have much sleep last night so I didn't feel good when I got up this morning. Even so, I had to drag myself because I had to go the studio this morning for my saxophone session.

I normally walk up the escalator without difficulty, with or without my saxophone. I was quite shocked. I stopped walking up half-way through. For some reason, this morning was a bit of a struggle for me to wake up.

'This is not me! This is not me at all!' I thought to myself.

I overheard someone talking about his long service leave of 35 weeks. That translates to approximately 40 years of service. That guy has been working with the same employer for 40 years. That's amazing! I admire this guy for his virtue of long suffering.

Did he suffer?

I like to make comparisons of things. This guy for example who worked for 40 years. If he bought coffee everyday on the way to work for 40 years (5 days a week), he would have had 10,400 cups of coffee. And say, the average coffee cost is $3.50, he could have saved $36,400. That's without even taking into account the power of compounding. He could have bought a brand new car with that money or even a deposit for a house.

Okay, let's not go there. Let's just stop right there.

On the tram home, this tram driver kept tapping the microphone. No announcements. It was quite annoying. If I were sitting at the front, I would have _____.

Oops!

There are offers, no takers

I offered a seat to a lady on the train to the city but she refused. So I took the seat instead. When the train was approaching Parliament Station, I got up to prepare.

Guess what happened next?

The lady whom I offered the seat to before took my seat. Maybe she got tired of standing. Some people don't like receiving offers. Some people like to give offers.

On the tram to work, I couldn't believe what I saw. I didn't know if this girl was just trying to be funny or if she was doing it out of habit. Okay, here is what she did. She was picking her nose while she was looking at me. She obviously wanted me to watch her pick her nose. I don't understand what's happened since I got on the train this morning. People have been acting in bizarre, crazy and gross ways.

On the train home, two teenagers who looked like lovers sat on the floor and started to talk intimately. Then they kissed. I didn't really want to watch them kissing so I looked away.

Give them some privacy.

Well, you can't really have privacy on the train, can you?

12th, Thursday

I pranked. She screamed. I laughed.

CAUTION: Do not attempt this!

I saw a friend-colleague this morning waiting for the pedestrian green man. She didn't see me. So I decided to pull a prank. I grabbed her bag forcefully from behind. I couldn't believe what happened next—she screamed. It was so loud I almost blew my ears off. She obviously didn't know it was me. When she turned around, she saw my serious, scared-to-death face. The people around us were dumbfounded, I didn't know what to do.

Then my friend started talking to me. She laughed. The people around us later realised it was a prank.

I laughed.

I was telling her how she scared me to death with her scream. I thought people were going to jump on me and beat me up.

I'll never do that again. It scared the crap out of me!

13th, Friday

Fashion tips

This guy who was in his 40s was wearing the teenagers' fashion, chino pants and matching t-shirt. At first, you wouldn't be able to tell that he is in his 40s. His outfit basically made him look like a twenty-year old. So, there you go. If you want to look younger, just wear what young people wear. I also noticed that wearing light-coloured shirts can also make you look younger.

Catching the public transport because of this book project definitely made me more observant. I picked up a lot of fashion trends.

16th, Monday

On my face

Some people just don't think or care about the impact of their actions on other people. They are completely oblivious of what's happening around them.

For example, this guy got on the tram and stood next to me with his backpack touching my face. It was absolutely annoying and it tested my patience. I was about to tell him off when a passenger got up to get off the tram. That's when he took a seat. Good!

I wore my eyeglasses to work today, I normally just use them when I drive. I'm not used to this. I might not wear them again at work. I'm short-sighted anyway so I don't really need them at work when I'm ten inches away from the computer.

17th, Tuesday

Mind over Tuesday

I couldn't sleep last night but somehow I felt good this morning. I was telling myself that I have things that needed to do today and today only, including updating my blogs.

On the tram, a boy's backpack was touching my face. This is the second day in a row that someone annoyingly touched my face. He didn't even realise he was doing it, unless of course he's pretending.

What's wrong with these people?

I exercised my self-control to the fullest today. I really wanted to give this boy a lecture about sensitivity but I kept telling my mind to just let it go.

So I did let it go.

18th, Wednesday

Brad Pitt

My tram was almost empty this morning. I couldn't believe it. For a moment, I thought I caught the wrong tram.

Then a group of girls got on the tram. They started staring at me. I felt like I was Brad Pitt by the way they look at me.

Seriously! Stop staring! Even if I'm Brad Pitt, you don't have to stare at a guy like there's no tomorrow. This is absolutely unbelievable!

On the train home, while I was writing my travel notes on my phone, I would occasionally look up the train ceiling. Then I noticed the guy standing a few metres would look at me every time I looked up. I looked back at him. We would stare at each other for a couple of seconds. This happened a few times so after like the seventh time, I never looked up. I just kept typing on phone until I got off the train.

Postcodes

There's this guy on the train who had an 'updo' hairstyle. I thought only women do 'updo.' He had a crazy goatee, black pair of pants and a plain white shirt. He was carrying a guitar. While I was sitting there he started playing air guitar conspicuously and everyone could see him.

While I was sitting inside the tram, I felt the urgent call of nature.

Crap! I didn't bring a plastic bag with me today.

I could not wait to get off the tram. Every second that went by seemed like eternity. Once the tram stopped and the doors opened, I ran to find the nearest public toilet. I was desperate. I eventually found one and went straight in. I was such in a rush that I missed to lock the toilet door once I was inside. I only realised that it was unlocked when I finished using it and got out. Luckily, no one came in. It would have been an eventful Thursday morning.

I walked to catch my tram stop when Yarra Trams announced that the trams were being diverted because of an ill passenger. This meant I had to walk two blocks to catch a connecting tram on Spencer Street. Hopefully, the passenger was fine.

On the way home, some girls were talking about the different Australian postcodes of each state. That Victoria (VIC) starts with 3; New South Wales (NSW) with 2; Queensland (QLD) with 4; South Australia (SA) with 5. They were unsure about Northern Territory (NT) and Tasmania (TAS), which are 8 and

7, respectively. Western Australia (WA) starts with 6. Australian Capital Territory (ACT) also starts with 2, same as NSW. There you go, some postcode trivia for today.

20th, Friday

Early Christmas shopping?

I sat next to an expectant lady on the train. There's something about expectant mothers that make me feel like I'm being re-energised. I know, it's weird. Don't ask me why.

While I was typing my travel notes on my phone, I realised that it was already towards the end of March. I felt like I only started this train commute book project not too long ago and now it's been almost six months. Time absolutely, unbelievably, crazily, ridiculously flies.

Soon it will be Christmas! I better start my Christmas shopping.

23rd, Monday

Tram girls are cuter?

I don't know if other guys would agree with me but I've noticed tram girls are cuter than the ones on the train. Maybe I should research this. I do a lot of reading on the train including catching up with my saxophone music lessons. Cute girls distract me. That's why it's a good thing that I don't bring my eyeglasses with me when I catch the public transport. I can better concentration.

The weather is a bit gloomy today but the temperature is not bad, 22°C. Talking about distraction, a girl kept looking or shall I say staring at me on the train home. I felt conscious.

I asked for no distraction this morning and all I got was a distraction. Unbelievable!

24th, Tuesday

Inexplicable

WARNING: The following may sound weird to you as it was to me when it happened, so don't be alarmed. You're not the only one. Until now I'm not sure whether I was just half asleep or hallucinating at that time. So here it is:

When I got to the train station and parked my car, I checked the time on my phone and saw that it was 7:02 in the morning. I thought, 'this can't be right. I left home at 7 am and warmed up my car. That takes at least three minutes. To drive to the station and look for a spot is another seven minutes. This means I should have been at the station by 7:10 A.M. Not 7:02 A.M. I disregarded the time calculation in my head and trusted my phone with the 7:02 A.M. time. To walk to the platform from the car park takes five minutes. This meant that I could make it to the platform by 7:07 am. I already missed the 7:03 and the next express train was 7:14. This meant that I had seven minutes to spare before the next train arrives. While I was walking down the stairs to the platform, I heard the announcement that that 7:14 train was departing.

What? You're kidding me. You cannot be serious man, you cannot be serious! It's only 7:07 A.M. I was literally complaining but not as loud as Maria

Sharapova. I rubbed my eyes making sure I was awake. I could feel I was awake. So what the!

When I got on the train, I felt very sleepy so and closed my eyes until the train arrived at Parliament Station.

I have to get my caffeine fix. What happened this morning at the train station was just weird and plainly inexplicable. Well, it's either me going crazy or the phone malfunctioned. I don't think that would happen to an iPhone. You guess!

25th, Wednesday

Female toilet

It's been so cold since last night so it was hard for me to get up this morning.

I put my winter jacket on. I'm freezing!

Everyone on the train was looking down on their phones so there is not much to share with you from this morning's journey.

My trip home, however, ended up in a female's toilet. So keep reading.

I was running towards Melbourne Central Station to catch the train. The escalator was broken so I took the stairs and because I was rushing I didn't pay much attention to the signs. I just kept running. I didn't realise that I was actually running towards the female toilet. When I got there, the ladies looked at me, confused and surprised. That's when I realised where I was. It was so embarrassing. I ran back upstairs with my head down.

I walked slowly towards the platform, read all the signs, and waited for the next train.

26th, Thursday

One Direction

Every Thursday, two girls would hand out *Review* weekly magazine outside Parliament Station. They speak Spanish.

'Buenas dìas preciosa!' I almost said what I was thinking.

On the train I was hearing this guy talking to the lady next to him about his apprenticeship that he's doing. He said he has been looking for a job but had no luck. He was almost giving up. The lady was trying to comfort him but he still went on and on about how hard it has been for him.

The rest of the passengers either were reading the *mX* or their phones. They were probably reading about Zayn Malik leaving the boy band One Direction. It's all over the social media. People have been asking why he was leaving and if the rest of the band will continue.

27th, Friday

Smoking wafer sticks

I was eating wafer sticks holding them like cigarettes. It looked like I was smoking wafer sticks. A schoolboy who was watching me probably thought I was crazy.

I was listening to this audio recording about embracing and overcoming pain to succeed; not waiting for the perfect time to do something but rather create it. Applying that to my wafer stick scenario would be something like this:

I'm not troubled by what people think or say about me or how I smoke my wafer sticks. I love my wafer sticks and nothing can take that away from me. You can take way my wafer sticks, maybe; but no one can take away my love for them.

Well, by the time I got off the train my stomach felt funny. Too much chilli from last night's dinner, wafer sticks, morning coffee—I don't think all of these would result to a funny stomach.

30th, Monday

Push

For some reason, I had a renewed desire to quit my job this year. There was a sudden rush of energy and I didn't know where it came from. I had so much energy that I decided not to take the tram and walked two blocks to get to work.

What the heck?

When I was trying to get on the tram, this well-dressed girl pushed me up the steps.

'Don't get me started girl, you haven't seen my bad side yet,' I thought.

Being in a hurry doesn't give you the license to push people.

I was running to catch the express train home and this guy on the right side of the escalator was walking very slowly.

'Hello! Can't you hear my footsteps pounding?' I thought, 'this guy is lucky.

If were the Matchbox Twenty girl on the tram who pushed people, he would have already been on the floor, by this time.

I finished a little bit early today at work so I got to get home earlier than usual. Though, I had to drive back to the city to do some more saxophone practice.

31st, Tuesday

Self-talk

A lady was talking to herself at the tram stop. A lot like myself. More often than not, I ask myself a lot of questions before I make decisions. However, this particular lady's self-talk was getting louder. Then I realised that she looked like she was suffering from a mental illness. I got on the tram and she followed me. She continued the self-talk inside the tram. Then, the following happened at one of the tram stops on Clarendon Street.

The tram driver had just closed the doors and was about to move the tram when this self-talking lady demanded that the doors be opened again as she wanted to get off. The tram driver was kind enough to re-open the doors for her.

I was standing, with my back leaning on a folded seat on the train. This girl with bags of groceries got on the train and I asked her if she wanted me to put the folded seat down so she could sit and she said yes. So we sat next to each other.

I wanted to do some computer work at Starbucks so I caught the tram back to the city. The tram was absolutely packed. A girl stepped on my toes with her high heels. That made me step and accidentally hit the guy standing behind me. He told me off. I apologised.

What can I do? You can't really tell him it was the fault of the girl who had the high heels who stepped on my toes.

Anyway, when I said sorry he calmed down.

APRIL

1ˢᵗ, Wednesday

The Exorcist

I had a very good sleep last night. For an insomniac like me, a very good sleep is a luxury. I got up with a renewed momentum and energy. Then I felt that I had to revisit my goals I set last year to see if I accomplished most of them.

I didn't even take notes of what people were doing on the train, except for one: the lady sitting next to me. I wasn't even sure if she was a lady. No. It's not what you think! I felt like I was sitting next to a robot. She didn't move a muscle. She blinked a few times and that's about it.

When I left work today, I felt a little bit sick. I didn't know how or why. I felt totally healthy earlier today and now I felt like crap all of a sudden. It must be the bad spirits from the movie *The Exorcist*. I told them to get out of my body.

Get out!

2nd, Thursday

Donald Duck

I got up feeling really sick. I took some Cold and Flu tablets with me just in case. I didn't really want to take a day-off from work. Easter long weekend starts tomorrow anyway so I would feel guilty if I didn't go to work today.

I don't know how I survived at work today. I don't think Cold and Flu tablets can replace rest. I am really looking forward towards the long-weekend, although I'm probably going to be resting anyway.

On the train home, I was sitting there like Donald Duck dozing off with a runny nose. I looked around to check if someone was looking at Donald Duck. No one was! Everyone was looking down on their phones. Nobody really cared about Donald Duck.

7th, Tuesday

I'm not Channing Tatum

It's weird getting up this morning to go to work after a four-day Easter weekend. I haven't fully recovered from the flu. So I wasn't back to my normal energetic, fast-walking and crazy state. Then I remembered what Anthony Robbins said that there is no difference between what you imagine and what you actually experienced. So I decided to put this to test. I tricked my mind and pretended that I am well and healthy.

It didn't work. Stuff it!

I was sitting on a tram when a girl started staring at me. I could see it in the corner of my eye. I tried not to look back at her. I let her enjoy the view of my face for a while. I'm not Brad Pitt. I'm not Channing Tatum, either. I don't know why girls stare at me. This girl must have forgotten her contact lenses.

Anyway, when she stared at me, it boosted my self-esteem.

Thanks girl!

I wonder what girls would feel when guys look at them. Would they feel like they were Angelina Jolie or Jennifer Lawrence?

8th, Wednesday

Diversity

If you want to experience Melbourne's diversity, just jump on the tram. You will see people with different nationalities (appearance), socio-economic levels (the way they dress), religious backgrounds (the way they dress as well), and whether they're employees (if they wear uniforms), students (if they carry books) or unemployed (this one is hard to tell). There are probably psychopaths as well. Who knows? Maybe the lady sitting next to you is a murderer.

This morning I didn't walk all the way up the escalator. I felt a bit unwell today. Normally I would walk up two sets of escalator at Parliament Station. Sometimes, I even pound my feet behind those who walk slower than me so they can hear me. Some of them get the message but most of them don't. That's when I start to make weird noises like '*arabarabarroo*' or '*bakalabadoo*.' Some people then turn around and give me either a frown or a confused look. I smile at them. Then they get more confused.

9th, Thursday

U-turn

My train was altered to run directly to Flinders Street. Again!

I went to Starbucks to rest for a bit. By this time I wasn't feeling too good. I was resting my head on the table and it wasn't good. I got out of Starbucks and went to the tram stop. I felt absolutely sick. I couldn't bear it anymore so I rang up work that I was not coming in. I needed to rest.

I caught the tram home.

Sometimes, even though your mind wants to do things, your body says otherwise. You need to listen. I'm guilty of this all the time. I often force myself often to do things that I sometimes forget to rest or eat. It's not a good idea. Perhaps you can skip meals once in a while, but making it a habit definitely has consequences.

I was on the tram home that morning and I was imagining my cosy room and warm bed. Nice!

10th, Friday

Open Sesame!

A well-dressed woman got on the train and started to walk back and forth the carriage trying to decide where to sit. There were literally quite a few empty seats. I don't know what kind of seat she was looking for. They're all the same to me.

Maybe she liked a seat that massages. Well, it ain't happening here lady.

I was standing on the tram and was coughing heavily. I felt helpless and embarrassed. I could hear my cough echo on the carriage. I tried to suppress it but my throat was really itchy. I should have just rested for another day.

There were tourists behind me who gave me a look while I was coughing. They probably thought, 'the heck is this guy doing, coughing his heart out? Come on man, take some medicine.'

Well, I did,' I replied in my head.

My tram travel was cut short when the driver announced that there was an ambulance in front of us because of a sick passenger. So I had to walk three blocks towards Spencer Street. I executed CSWW—Coughing and Sneezing While Walking.

After work I went to Southern Cross to catch the train from there. I wanted to get a seat and so I stood there right behind the line so when the train stopped I was the first to get on board. However, an embarrassing thing happened. When the train came to a full stop, I pressed the button but it didn't open. I pressed it again but still didn't work. I thought the door was broken. Meanwhile, I was holding up the people behind me who were waiting to get on the train. I pressed it for the third time and nothing happened. I was getting both frustrated and angry. I didn't know what was going on with the train or myself. I was so angry that I pushed the button so hard with my fist that it opened for the fourth time.

Tra-la! When I was inside the train I realised that I was still not well enough. My body was still weak. Fortunately, it's Friday and that means I can rest throughout the weekend.

Open Sesame!

Taylor Swift and pancit

I brought some food on the train for my lunch. It was a homemade Filipino dish called *pancit* that my brother cooked on the weekend. It was in a see-through lunchbox and everyone could see it on the train.

This guy in particular was staring at my lunchbox and no matter how many times I tried to look at him to send a gentle message: *'Your stare at my lunchbox makes me feel a little bit* _____,' he ignored it.

I must admit *pancit* is really yummy. Well, the guy didn't say 'please' so I didn't give him any. Thou shalt not ask and thou shalt not be given.

I was facing towards the front of the tram when I saw half of a girl's face that looked like Taylor Swift. *Love Story, Shake It Off, You Belong With Me.* These are just some of the songs that make me happy. She was looking out the window so I couldn't see her whole face.

When she turned around, I realised she was a forty-seven year old woman. She was basically an older version of Taylor Swift.

Oh well, I was still happy.

14th, Tuesday

My honey

Okay, my morning was again greeted by a guy sitting on a priority seat with crossed legs with his umbrella sitting next to him.

Not really.

I jumped on the and there were only two blokes and four women. More people joined us at Spencer Street station.

Come in guys. Join us. The more the merrier. Like what Pharrell Williams said 'Clap along if you feel like a room without a roof because I'm happy.

I was happy until I left work today. I carried my honey today. I held her in my hands. She is my sweetie! I met her at Woolworths this morning. I'm talking about the real Capilano honey in a bottle. Thank you honey!

On the train home, a guy got on from a city look station with a guide dog. I wasn't sure if he was blind because he was guiding his dog where to sit instead of him being guided by the dog. It's like sitting on the driver's seat and being driven by the car.

Perhaps, he was training the dog to be a guide dog.

Who knows?

15th, Wednesday

Full-time hobby

I sat next a girl who was playing games on her phone. I tried to look over to see what she was playing but as soon as she saw me looking, she stopped playing. Then, she closed her phone and put it down.

How rude?

I saw a video last night about this 60-year-old man who plays video games full-time. He would go to this video centre every day competing with teenagers and kids. He would take a break for an hour and come back to his game. He would beat younger players. That's how he earned their respect. Even the teenagers who were interviewed for the video praised his old man's abilities in computer games despite his age.

When I got off the train to go out of Parliament Station, I could see some passengers standing at the bottom of the stairs. They were looking up like someone or something was about to fall. My curiosity grew as I walked towards them. When I got to the bottom of the stairs, I looked up. It was the rain! And these people don't have umbrellas and they didn't want to get wet. I didn't want to get wet either. So I stood there waiting for the rain to stop. After a few minutes, I ran out of patience. I ran as fast as I could to the tram stop. I didn't care if I got wet.

When I got on the tram, this blonde girl sitting opposite to me was busy writing some notes while making glances once a while. I got a feeling she could be the female version of me working on another travel diary. How funny it would be if I get my book published about my train and tram travels and she does too. One of her entries is about me and my entry for today is about her. By this time, the sun came out all of a sudden. Oh Melbourne, I love your unpredictability! It was raining a few minutes ago and now it's sunny.

On the train home, four friends were sitting closely to each other talking. Three were plus size and one skinny. I wonder whether the three would influence the skinny to become plus size or the skinny one to inspire the plus size to be skinny. Well, it is three against one. You tell me.

A girl got on the train before Box Hill Station and she instantly caught my attention because she was wearing multi-coloured leggings. I call it rainbow leggings.

Men don't wear leggings but I don't think I would wear rainbow pants either. I don't know what happened to our fashion. It's gone completely _____.

16th, Thursday

Flip

I was sitting at the platform seat when I saw a lady wearing a Sony Walkman. That's like a twenty-year-old technology. I didn't even know that people still use them.

I got on the train and sat opposite to the girl I sat next to yesterday. It looked like she was wearing the same outfit—blue New Balance rubbers shoes, pair of grey slack pants, black jacket and green-black backpack. She also had eyeglasses on.

When I caught my connecting tram, I tried to lean on the wall right next to a girl. She then moved away and sat down.

What the heck? Do I smell? I take a shower every day and spray LYNX every morning!

On the way to work, someone pressed the Next Stop button three times while the tram was at a stop. So the driver kept the door open for a while but no one got off.

Someone was just playing around with the tram cord. This was on a morning peak hour.

Now this was the highlight of the day. A guy pulled out something from his pocket. It didn't look like it was very long. I was wondering what it was. When it was finally out, I realised it was a flip phone. My last recollection about flip phones was six or seven years ago when I still had my Motorola flip phone. I was flipping my phone playfully when it broke. I made my last flip and that was it.

17th, Friday

Profanity

A girl was practising some dance moves on the platform but she stopped when she saw me approaching. I kept walking until I was at the middle of the platform. When I turned around I saw her continue her dancing. Funny girl.

I have a favourite spot at the waiting bay where once the train stops, I'm directly in front of the door of the carriage close to the Parliament Station exit. I calculated what carriage I need to be on so I can get out of the station quickly.

An elderly woman got on the tram. I got up and offered my seat but she refused.

Okay fine.

There were also quite a few empty seats. Maybe she just liked standing. The only issue was she wasn't holding onto anything at all. So when the tram stopped, she almost fell.

'Oops! Are you alright ma'am?' I asked.

Luckily, I was behind her so I was able catch her.

Another elderly woman was about to get off the tram and she was getting directions from a guy. And because she was at the door, she was holding up people who were about to board the tram. People could see what was happening and they were patient enough to wait until she understood the instructions. At the same time, I could see the impatience in their faces. If they don't hurry, the tram may close the door and they would have to wait for the next one.

Three teenage boys got on at Southern Cross. They started talking and one of them seemed to have a speech problem. He was stammering a lot. As I listened to their conversation, the boys started to swear, particularly the one who was stammering. He literally used the F word to describe every word in the sentence. I felt like telling these boys to calm down. Well, they got off at Richmond Station anyway so at least I didn't have to hear all the swearing all the way home. Otherwise, today's entry would be full of profanity.

18th, Saturday

Be warned!

I went to university today to do some readings for my tax studies—a lot of boring cases and legislation. After that, I caught the tram from Carlton to Melbourne Central and this guy started staring at me from when I got on until I got off at Melbourne Central. It was creepy! He wore a black suit, brown hat and a pair of jeans. I tried to memorise his outfit for some strange reason. So next time you see someone stare at you and he's wearing the outfit that I just described, be warned!

20th, Monday

Hold the rail

I missed my train so I had to catch next express train. The second express train was packed but I managed to get a seat. It was because of this nice girl who moved to give me more room so I could sit comfortably.

'Coffee?' I thought.

She had this really great smile. That definitely made my day. I felt I was going to melt at that moment, like M&M's chocolates.

It made me realise that oftentimes we underestimate the power of little acts of kindness we do every day. Little things like a smile, offering seats on the train, catching elderly people before they fall like what happened the other day, and list goes on.

On the train home, a lady with carrier bags on both arms got on from the city loop and stood next to the door. She wasn't holding onto a rail so every time the train stopped she would end up a few metres from her previous spot. It was both painful and ridiculous to watch.

'Why couldn't she just hold the rail? Just put down the bags of stuff and hold the grab rail for your safety. No one's going to steal you bags of stuff,' I felt like telling her off.

21st, Tuesday

Ramp

I was on the tram on the way to work this morning when I saw a hermit getting off a tram. He was in a hurry. He had very long hair, thick and unkempt beard and was carrying a big, heavy backpack. Then I had this thought:

What if I go to some mountain and live there for a year. What would I have become after that time? I would probably have long, curly hair and a beard. I would probably get better at playing saxophone because I would have all the time to practise.

I was looking at the overhead tram announcement screen for the tram arrival times when this lady looked at me. She thought I was looking at her.

'Sorry lady, you don't need to give me that nasty look because I ain't looking at you,' I thought.

A disabled guy on his electric wheelchair got on at Flagstaff Station. The train driver normally puts the ramp down for disabled people. There are train drivers just drop the ramp on the floor that everyone could hear. Oftentimes, it gives me a fright when they do this. Seriously, I don't know what's with some drivers that literally slam the ramp too loud. It's absolutely unbelievable.

22nd, Wednesday

Break the rules

This morning was one of those uninteresting days. Everyone was well-behaved on the train. There is nothing to talk about. Then, I remember this video of Arnold Schwarzenegger giving a commencement speech. He said you need to 'break the rules' to succeed. He said that people around you may impose rules on how you should act or behave. It's like being stuck in a box. Anyway, this 'break the rules' encouragement by Arnie doesn't apply to how you behave on the train. I mean you can't really break the rules and write graffiti on the train.

I'm just being silly as I try to apply it out of context.

I caught a guy staring at me, who later looked away. While he was looking away, I was looking at him. When he turned he saw me looking at him, so I looked away. That was awkward. I think he likes me.

Just joking.

A girl was drinking her can of beer while waiting for the tram. She looked like a university student.

Hey girl! Have you done your assignments yet?

23rd, Thursday

Casino

While I was waiting for my train at the platform, this lady announcer kept reminding passengers a number of times to stay behind the yellow line; let the passengers exit the train first before boarding the train; and to move in as far as you can once on the train. It was quite annoying actually. A reminder announcement is good but to repeat it quite a few times is sometimes irritating.

I went to do some saxophone lessons this morning. After sax, I went to catch my tram. I almost didn't get on because the tram was packed. When the tram stopped, I was right in front of the door when it opened so I jumped on straight away. I felt guilty because the ladies who were at the stop waiting before me were not able to board the tram.

An elderly man caught my tram at Batman Park stop. He pulled something out of his pocket—bundle of cash and he started counting it. Then he got off the Casino tram stop. You know what's going to happen next. He's going to buy a bowl of chips and watch the pigeons along the Yarra River. At 11 A.M. he's going to get his usual soy cappuccino and sip it while watching the pigeons again along the Yarra River on the west side. And of course after lunch, he would gamble at the casino until midnight.

What the heck am I talking about? Just ignore me. I have too much imagination.

On the way home, there was a bit of a drama. A guy at the tram stop screamed at the top of his lungs while the tram stopped near the Casino. Everyone on the tram got scared. We looked around to see if the guy was going to get on the tram. Once the tram doors closed, everyone had a sign of relief.

No one knew why or what it was about.

24th, Friday

Tramcar restaurant

A guy on the train sneezed a few times without covering his mouth. I was standing about two meters away from him. This is how you get sick on a public transport system. People are generous enough to pass the virus onto others.

Nice!

These two mates were talking about how they love school and how they love their postgraduate courses. They even plan to take their careers further and take doctorate degrees.

I was standing there wondering what they were doing to their human lives.

Don't get me wrong. Studying is great and I love studying myself. But I think unless you start applying what you've studied you won't be able to produce anything. I think before you continue to pursue your next degree, you may need to gain some experience first to apply and validate some of the theories you've learned so far. You can then use the results from the experience to further investigate some of the theories that you've learned and practised.

On the way home while I was walking towards the tram stop I could see the tram coming so I walked faster. As I was approaching the tram, I noticed I was the only one eager to board the tram. The rest were still standing at the tram stop. When the tram stopped I realised that it was a tramcar restaurant—not a passenger tram. Not one but two of them.

27th, Monday

Coloured

I sat next to the girl I've been sitting next to in the last two weeks. She was wearing pretty much the same outfit. Okay, perhaps we should give her the benefit of the doubt. She might have ten pairs of pants of the same colour, seven coats of the same design and five pairs of similar types of sneakers.

On the tram to work, this lady who was sitting near the aisle of the tram on a two-seater. She didn't want to move to the window seat so I squeezed myself in so I could get to the window seat. It was fine by me because I have minuscule body anyway. If were the lady I would have moved because the tram was packed and it would help if passengers who were already on the tram to move in as far as they could to give way to the passengers who are getting on. Anyway, that's my whinge for today.

28th, Monday

Flower jumper

I was preparing to get off the train in the city loop when a very tall guy got up. He instantly caught my attention because he was wearing a green-striped jumper with a flower design. He looked like an office worker because he wore a pair of slacks and leather shoes and was carrying a briefcase.

Is this what you call _____?

The last time I used the word _____ was never. And this is the first time I'm using it. I just can't help it. Perhaps, the only good thing about being a _____ is that you stand out from the crowd. You get attention. So next time you need care and attention, just wear a completely colour-uncoordinated outfit. I guarantee you will get noticed.

A teenage boy on the tram was wearing really tight jeans. I just hoped that his testicles don't get squashed. I don't know about these tight jeans, folks. Try to protect your assets please.

On the train home, a guy was working on his laptop was staring at me. I actually didn't realise he was looking at me until I took my earphones off my ears. I was off with the fairies while listening to Michael Jackson. He probably thought I was a snub.

Oh well, why would a guy stare at another guy anyway?

I smiled at him before I got off the train.

29th, Tuesday

Hammer

I caught an early train this morning. 6:49 A.M.! I was still cleaning the corners of my eyes as I waited at the platform.

I got on the train and saw a well-dressed man in the corner priority seat with crossed legs. It was obvious he didn't want anyone to sit next to him.

Well, he met the exception this morning. I could see there is a little gap between his leg that was sticking out and the wall. So I squeezed myself into the gap, brushing against his long leg. He then uncrossed his legs.

Thank you, Sir.

Everyone on the train was either reading or watching about the two Australians who were executed in Indonesia. I just prayed for the families of Andrew Chan and Myuran Sukumaran during this difficult time. I saw the paintings of Myuran online and I must admit his works of art are amazing. What a waste of such a great talent. The tension between Australia and Indonesia is at its highest today. Some people even called for boycotting Bali.

I was on the tram, looking out the window when the man's phone rang and he was sitting next to me. It was the loudest phone ring I have ever heard in my entire life. If I brought my hammer today, I would have smashed that phone into pieces.

Just joking.

A lady was walking towards the train door to prepare to get off Camberwell Station. The only problem was that she was facing the wrong side of the train. It was the side towards the train tracks not the platform. When the train stopped, the lady tried to open the door. Of course it wouldn't open. I suspect that she was either very hungry or just trying to be funny. I told her to face the other side—the platform side. She said it was hard to see as it was already dark.

30th, Wednesday

Prowl

I can't believe it's the last day of April. Where has the New Year's Day gone? Eight more months before next Christmas!

I got on the train this morning and stood next to a guy with his head sticking out. I was wondering what he was up to. Then I realised he was prowling on other passengers. He would stick his head out of his seat to hear these two teenage girls' conversation. He would read the paper for a few seconds then continue to prowl on other people again. It was not very pleasant to watch. Everyone could see what he was doing. When he turned to listen to these two girls again, it was obvious he wasn't going to stop anytime soon. He didn't actually need to stick his head out if all he wanted was to listen to the conversation because I could also hear their conversation although I was a few of metres away. They were just talking about their accounting classes and boys at university.

On the train home, I felt like I was at Victoria market. I could hear people speak in at least five different languages. I recognised only three—Vietnamese, Mandarin and English. The other two sounded European. Listening to them was like listening to Guns N' Roses, Jason Mraz and Adele at the same time.

MAY 2015

1st, Friday

Fight of the century

I was so excited about the Pacquiao-Mayweather boxing fight of the century on Sunday afternoon which will be Saturday night in Las Vegas. I got up early this morning and caught the 6:05 A.M. train to the city. I had a radio program at 7 A.M. so I shared my excitement to the listeners as well. Everyone at the studio talked a lot about the upcoming fight and I think even for those people who don't normally watch boxing will probably find themselves watching the fight on Sunday.

For some reason I felt that there were more passengers on the early train this morning than it used to be couple of months ago. Maybe people have new jobs in the city or maybe they just like to be early. One of the passengers was a plus size guy who was dozing off. Then a plus size lady got on the train and sat next to the plus size guy. There wasn't much room left but she still tried to squeeze her body in. Although she was sitting opposite me I tried not to look at her face. I looked away but I could see in the corner of my eye that she was giving me a nasty look. She crossed her arms.

On the train home on my right, I saw a guy playing Candy Crush on his iPhone. I haven't seen a guy playing Candy Crush before.

Most of my Facebook friends who invited me to play Candy Crush were female.

That's okay Olay, keep playing. Don't worry about me.

On my left was a guy on Skype talking to his mate like there's no tomorrow. Everyone could hear him and because I was sitting close to him I felt like my ears were going to burst. So I put my headphones on. I had peace.

4th, Monday

Sensitivity

The list of selfish people occupying the whole two-seater seat is growing at an exponential rate. There were two already on my morning train. I was standing there looking at both of them hoping one of them would move so I could sit. Nothing happened. One of them just kept reading his iPad.

I still kept thinking about the Pacquiao-Mayweather fight on the weekend and I could feel I've got a few punches in me waiting to be unleashed. This is what happens when you watch too many boxing on YouTube. To be honest, it wasn't the quality of fight I was expecting. People thought that it could have been more exciting if Pacquiao threw more punches and if Mayweather didn't run away too much. It was difficult to tell who the better boxer was, even though Mayweather was declared the winner.

On the tram home, a couple were arguing about the house they were moving into. I didn't mind overhearing their argument. I was more annoyed by the guy who had his backpack on my face.

He didn't even realise he was doing it because he was too busy arguing with his girlfriend.

That's okay, I forgive you whoever you are! Have some sensitivity next time!

5th, Tuesday

Gloomy

I ran to the platform this morning to make it to the 7:17 A.M. train. And I did. I was as determined as Manny Pacquiao. I still have the boxing hangover. I don't know how long this is going to last so I better use this as motivation to get myself into doing exercises again. Thank you Manny.

Every time it rains, everything seems to run slow. It affects people's moods as well. People don't seem to smile often. It looks gloomy outside and it' affecting me. Somehow I need to find a way to cheer myself up particularly now that the winter is just around the corner.

6th, Wednesday

Eyeglasses

I must admit I haven't been observing passengers much because I have a tax assignment due tomorrow. I was sitting on the train trying to juggle between reading tax cases and watching other passengers. I couldn't see clearly as I didn't have my eyeglasses on. It was good in a way because I was not distracted much by the pretty girls. Although I caught a girl staring at me twice. I tried not to be flattered because I had to finish my assignment.

And since I could not see her face clearly, I assume she was cute based on the contour of her face. I wonder how many ladies look at me when I'm not wearing my eyeglasses. There could be dozens! Just kidding. I don't know where I got this narcissistic attitude in me today.

7th, Thursday

Fashionable

This morning was my last chance to finish my tax assignment. After I answered the last question, I had a deep sigh of relief. It was freedom once again! I read a few articles about Pacquiao and Mayweather and there was a talk of a rematch next year after Pacquiao gets his surgery and rehabilitation. For the benefit of those who didn't know, it was reported after that fight of the century on the weekend that Manny Pacquiao had injured his shoulder before the fight and that it required surgery. He will also have to be rehabilitated and be out of the boxing scene for 8-9 months.

I saw this cute girl again on the tram to work. She had a sporty outfit today. I quite like how she puts on different styles. I don't see her everyday but when I do she always looks fashionable. It occurred to me that fashion is a multi-billion dollar industry and brands like H&M and Uniqlo are making millions if not billions of dollars in revenues worldwide. I had this crazy thought of starting my own shirt company.

Where do I start?

I was standing in the middle of a guy and a woman talking about her being a freelancer until an opportunity comes up.

Isn't freelancing already an opportunity anyway?

8th, Friday

Gentle driver

A girl wearing a scarf with an American flag design kept moving on a moving train. Come on girl, hold the rail. I saw that by the way she was moving that she could fall anytime. Instinct told me to stand next to her. She didn't fall.

For some reason I started sweating while standing on the train. So I took off my coat. I didn't know if it was internal hotness or what.

I walked as fast as humanly possible to the Collins Street tram stop to make it in time for my tram to work. It took me two minutes which I normally do in four. I feel that I still have the boxing hangover after watching last week's Fight of the Century.

With this next one, I don't know if I'm going to laugh or be annoyed.

On the train home, someone farted and the passengers near me kept looking at each other trying to suss out who the heck released the gas. The lady sitting opposite me gave me a nasty look.

What the heck? It wasn't me okay!

I was sitting there wondering who farted. I had a feeling it was the guy standing next to me. He was quiet. He was looking down and seemed to be focused on his iPhone. After a few stops he started to move a few metres away.

Man, it was definitely you, but they were looking at me! Come back here!

Two university students got on the train on my way home. I knew they were students by their conversation. One of them was barefooted. It was freezing and he was barefooted. I don't know what is happening to our youth these days.

A disabled man got off the train and the train driver who put the ramp down for the disabled man was very gentle. I didn't hear a sound. I just wish all drivers are like him. Normally it would be a very loud sound that you would scare the crap out of you.

11th, Monday

B. O.

I was standing on the train when the guy next to me pulled out something from his pocket. It was surgical mask. He put it on and then looked at me.

Excuse me?

I was wondering if I had B.O. today. I'm pretty sure I had a thorough shower. I also sprayed some deodorant and perfume.

What else do I need?

I have seen a few people wear mouth masks in the city as well. Not long after the trip the guy took the mask off when we arrived in the city.

What's the point of having it on if you're going to take it off anyway? I mean what's the difference between the air in the city and the air in Camberwell? And as I said before, I don't have B.O.

He could be suffering from a cold and he didn't want to spread it. Or he could be healthy and didn't want to get sick from other passengers' germs.

By the way did you know that wearing mouth mask or surgical mask, whatever you want to call it, is common in Japan?

12th, Tuesday

Trying

I was running to make it to my train. I made it to the platform and jumped on the train in a split second just before the train doors were shut. Thanks to this lady who held me up on the escalator.

It started to trickle while I was waiting for the tram at the stop. Someone actually slipped at the tram stop trying to make it before the tram doors closed. Everyone was like 'Oh!' He got up and climbed up the tram steps. He looked fine. I hope he was okay. Once the tram started to move, the driver reminded passengers to take extra care as it can be very slippery when it rains; and not to worry if you miss the tram because there will always be another one behind. Poor guy, he slipped and got told off. It was a general reminder but I think mainly for him.

It was the coldest night ever. I finished work and walked towards the tram stop. It was like walking through a vacuum of ice, if there is such a thing. It felt like I was in the desert. Yes, that's right desert of ice.

13th, Wednesday

Older ladies

I thought I saw Judi Dench on the train this morning. She was wearing a red coat. I never saw her catch a train in any of the 007 James Bond movies. It would be too risky for her. Hopefully, that coat is bullet proof.

I offered a seat to an older lady but completely ignored me as if she saw nothing.

What the heck?

Anyway, I didn't really worry too much about that because this is not the first that this happened to me. I've been ignored a few times mostly by older ladies.

Perhaps they didn't like my hair?

Well, I don't have much hair now anyway. I lost a few strands when I started writing this book.

14th, Thursday

There's always another one behind

I missed my train this morning so I waited for the next one. I also missed my tram, so I caught another one. Don't worry about missing your train or tram. There's always another one behind. This was the lesson I learned the other day when a man slipped and fell while running to catch the tram.

This lady on the tram was talking on the phone with someone saying that people in her life always cook for — her sister, mother and neighbour.

What more could she ask for? I'd like to be that person's neighbour too. Hey lady, where do you live?

On the train home, a guy was eating his apple while reading the *mX* paper. He then stuck the leftover on the edge of his seat.

'Come on man, if it's your house would you just leave your rubbish around?

Well, maybe he does,' I thought.

15th, Friday

Private and confidential

Two guys were talking about offenders' jail terms on the train. Sounded like they were parole officers. I don't think they should really be talking about those things in public. Those are confidential and sensitive information. Be mindful about this when you're in public places including public transport. When you share these sort of information in public, it reflects on what type of professional you are, if you can be called one. I thought that was all I wanted to say today.

Girls A and B

I didn't get my favourite spot on the train today, which is the middle carriage. By getting this carriage, I'd be closer to the exit points. But because I took the first carriage, it took me longer than usual to exit the station. There were new MYKI readers at Parliament Station. You tap on the screen instead of the plastic reader. I was confused at first because with the old one they use the screen to show your myki balance. Now, you tap on the screen itself. That's great that they did this because the old myki reader was sometimes not sensitive enough. On a few occasions I had difficulties with it that it wasn't reading my myki card at all. Meanwhile, I was holding up the people behind me.

On the train home, these two girls were having a bit loud conversation. Let's call them Girls A and B. Girl A was sitting next to a guy who was busy on his phone. I was on the next opposite seat and I could hear them. So I felt sorry for the guy who was next to them. Every time they mention a very private matter, this guy would look up and frown. Girl B was saying to Girl A how she liked her gym outfit to be tight to emphasize her _____. I don't want to go into the details of the conversation but Girl A prefers white skirt and that she likes to borrow her cousin's Converse.

Okay, let's just stop right here!

19th, Tuesday

Whoever that guy was

While I was waiting for my tram on Bourke Street, I saw a homeless guy smoking a cigar. The smell wasn't bad actually. I was curious about the difference between cigars and cigarettes. So I looked it up online. Apparently the probability of getting cancer from smoking cigars is higher compared to cigarettes. It could be because it's meant to be savoured on a longer smoking time.

I finished late at work so I was rushing to catch my train home. I was running down the escalator to catch the train when doors shut on my face. The man standing inside tried to press the button to open the door but it was too late. I had to wait for the next one. Thanks anyway whoever that guy was.

On the train home, a guy started to play his guitar with some instrumental music. The guitar wasn't tuned properly, so that wasn't really a pleasant experience on the way home. Someone started talking to him that's when he stopped. Thank you whoever that guy was — the guy who talked to the guitarist.

20th, Wednesday

This is so not me

I almost forgot to write travel notes today. I'm not sure if I already mentioned this but I was beginning to realise that watching what other passengers do on the train or tram and listening to conversation is not really my thing. The whole point of this travel book project was to make my daily commute interesting. My whole journey so far with this project has been quite interesting so I have achieved my goal in that regard. However, to keep checking on other passengers and listening to conversations is not something I would keep doing. Fortunately, this is just a project and not a lifestyle. Otherwise, I would go insane.

21ˢᵗ, Thursday

Cat food

I saw these on an older corporate-looking man: Marley headphones, D&G fashionable eyeglasses and unkempt hair. It would have been great if he had tidy hair. That would have been three green ticks.

I caught the tram to university after work to attend to my tax class. They were both boring — the journey and the class.

Though, going home on the tram was bit more interesting.

I got on the tram and the girl in front me made a loud comment that everyone could hear, 'It smells cat food in here!'

I became curious myself so I looked around to see if someone had cat food. I didn't see anyone with cat food. What I saw was this guy eating fish and chips, not cat food. He was looking down. He must have heard the girl's comment and thought that it was him. So it looked like he was trying to hide, avoiding to be discovered.

Why would fish and chips smell like cat food anyway? What the heck!

22nd, Friday

What I meant was...

It's Friday and I expected that everyone to be happy on the train.

Don't give me frowns. No sad faces. No fake braces, please! Just big smiles.

Well, it was a quiet tram to South Melbourne. There were only a couple of passengers. I could sit anywhere I liked. I quite enjoy when there's no one on the tram.

I don't know what I've eaten this morning or what sort of air I breathed today because on the train home, for some strange reason, I kept looking around and other passengers noticed and I could see some eyebrows raised. It looked like it was my first time to catch a train and I felt like playing around a bit. Then a blonde girl got on the train and sat next to me. More eyebrows were raised.

Why?

What?

24th, Sunday

Man leggings? Really?

I didn't actually have to write about my travels today because it is Sunday and Sunday is supposed to be a day of rest. However, I need your opinion about something I saw on the tram today.

I went to the city to do some work at Starbucks. After a few hours, I caught a tram back to my car. At the back of the tram a guy wearing leggings and a longline T-shirt reaching his knees. He was carrying a dog cage with a puppy in it obviously. His pair of shoes had heels as thick as the fog on a cold winter morning. It was a very interesting scene for me. I mean just picture this in your head—leggings, dog cage, puppy, longline shirt and thick shoes.

Is this the new fashion for guys?

25th, Monday

Smile and shoes

I was standing on the train when this strange-looking guy started to smile at me. Well, at least that's what I thought. So I smiled back. He frowned.

What the heck?

Then I realised he was smiling at someone behind me, over my shoulder. He would stop smiling for a few seconds, and would then smile again. He did it again and again. The whole scene felt schizophrenic. It felt like watching one of Jerry Seinfeld's shows about fading smiles. Look it up on YouTube.

I tried to smile back again at him but he returned me with frowns instead. Then I stopped smiling at him.

I don't know if he was just playing around with me or just being a plain _____.

I always take the right lane going up the escalator at Parliament Station. It's hard work. I reckon that is the longest escalator of all the train stations in Melbourne. I was checking out people's shoes while walking up. Different types of shoes worn by different types of creatures. Some of them were very dirty and there were only a few clean ones. I found that most guys had relatively clean shoes than girls.

It was an interesting observation this morning. Does that mean men clean their shoes more often than women? I certainly don't clean my shoes every week. I would just wear different pairs every day. I remember I used to wear just one pair of shoes every day for a year until it wore out.

When I got on the tram to work, people were either looking down or out the window with sad faces, like they were almost crying.

It's Monday, what do you expect?

26th, Tuesday

Two stares

The trains were delayed this morning, so I had to wait for a bit. While I was waiting, this strange-looking guy holding a take-away coffee cup was staring at me like crazy. I started to feel uncomfortable, so I walked away towards the other platform which I didn't really want to do because the train was due to arrive in a moment.

The trams were delayed as well so I had to walk a couple of blocks to get the tram. Before I got off the tram, this girl started at me very intently like I was going to melt. It scared the crap out of me.

Who the heck is the girl?

I couldn't wait to get out of that tram. Maybe she just liked me. Nice! I should have winked at her.

27th, Wednesday

Flannelette

I locked eyes with an attractive girl at the tram stop. Another awkward moment. We got on the tram together. While I was looking at her, she pulled out her phone and started texting. That's when I saw the wedding ring on her finger. My heart stopped beating for two seconds. Then I looked away.

'Somebody help me! That's okay Renelo. Take it easy! You'll find another one,' these voices in my head were driving me crazy.

These days flannelette shirts are becoming more fashionable. I don't know if you would agree with me but I think in the past if you wear one of those, people would think you're either dag or troublemaker. They kept a distance. These days, more and more people are wearing them, including women. I might actually get one for myself.

28th, Thursday

Come sit on my lap

I got on the train today and I saw the lady who walked away when I sat next to her a couple of months ago. I didn't know if she recognised me. Sometimes I think I should take a photo of her and include in this book. She made my train travel interesting.

When I caught the tram to work, a girl sitting on the priority seat wanted her boyfriend to sit on her lap. She was tapping her lap trying to get her man to sit but he refused. Of course, he did. I mean I would refuse too if I were the guy and if I have a girlfriend. Problem is I don't have one.

On the train home, this guy was talking very loudly on the phone in a strange language. Anyway, it was quite annoying that I had to turn my music volume up. Sometimes it makes me think that talking on the phone on the train to some people is such an enjoyable activity that it feels like eating ice cream with some nuts and blueberries on top of the Eiffel tower on a cold winter night.

29th, Friday

Hair

Every time I see another musician, it brings back memories of my early music journey. On the train to the city, I was sort of looking at this cute Asian girl with her cello while she was on the phone. She exuberates a different kind of aura that was almost magnetic. I became inspired. The more I became inspired, the more I glanced at her. Then, more music memories came back to me. By this time I was beginning to miss my saxophone practices. Lately, I was spending more time on this book and my other projects and less or no time for saxophone practices. This girl just reminded me of all my music I've done so far. Thank you girl.

I was waiting for the tram when I saw an ad about free Wi-Fi on board a Skybus. Behind the ad were three mature women on tracksuits staring at me. I think that's what it was. I wasn't wearing my eyeglasses so I couldn't tell.

'Really? Me? I don't think so. I already told you I'm no Brad Pitt. So please stop staring at me.

I was blushing while talking to myself. So I looked away.

Luckily, I wasn't wearing my eyeglasses, otherwise I would have been so distracted with all these ads that I would not have been able to catch the tram to work.

On the tram were two teenage girls having an entertaining conversation. One of them was sharing about her dreams last night of her having short hair on one side and long hair on the other side and how she kept brushing the side that has the longer hair. My morning was spent listening to this conversation about hair. She talked about her brother's afro hair and how he eventually got rid of it. By the time I got to work and turned my computer on all I that was in my head was hair.

30th, Saturday

Suitcase

Tramming on a Saturday morning is not normally a particularly exciting adventure. This morning was different. I caught the Tram 11 on Brunswick Street to the city after I got tired of waiting for Tram 86 on Smith Street. Thanks to the TramTracker app. It shows you the nearby tram stops so you have more journey options. It saves you time and energy.

I caught a tram on Elizabeth Street and this well-dressed African lady with wheeled suitcase was behind me. She had a nose ring and as you may know in their culture either represents marriage or wealth depending on which tribe you belong. She stood next to me on a packed tram and I felt weird. I felt her command for respect, like if she wanted something it was going to get done no matter what. It was a weird feeling and she didn't even say a single word.

I went to do some saxophone practice. My teacher was away for two weeks so I was all by myself at the studio. Every time I hit the high notes with funny sounds (to the saxophone players you know what I mean) I remember my teacher's frowning face telling me to keep practising every day. He knew by the way I played the sax that I didn't have enough practice for the week's lesson.

I caught the tram back to the city again after the sax session. By this time it was mid-afternoon and the people on the tram looked so relaxed. The ladies' faces looked like they were going to see Michael Buble. The guys looked like they were going to _____. It was all good and happy until this very tall girl got on board and stood next to me. Nice, just nice lady! You made me look really small.

31st, Sunday

Spiderman

It's Sunday and I'm back in the city again. I just love Melbourne. Coming here every day is like seeing my good old friend named Harry. His dad was the founder of a company called Oscorp. I went to their house once and met a girl named Gwen. She was beautiful. We went to the same school. Both of us were also good in science.

One day, I got bitten by a spider. The next day, I found myself jumping off one building after another using spider web that was coming out of my wrist.

Of course, I'm joking. I'm not Spiderman.

It's been cold and raining since I left this morning. Just the perfect way to get inspired.

Of course, I'm being sarcastic. I have to catch a tram to Brunswick to meet a friend and I can't use my web. The web shooter hasn't been working and today it is stuck frozen.

Thanks Melbourne.

JUNE 2015

1st, Monday

Hugs and kisses

It rained as soon as I left home this morning. Perfect timing. My train station is one of the good ones because parking is in the basement so even if it's pouring rain outside, you won't get wet. That's probably one of the reasons it gets full quickly during the week so you need to be really early if you want to get a parking spot.

On the tram home, I was standing near the myki reader. I was looking blankly at the people passing by. I was pretty tired by this time. I couldn't wait to get home. A couple got on the tram and stood next to me. After a few seconds they started embracing each other rubbing each other's body. After two stops another couple got on and also stood next to me. When they saw what the other couple were doing they also started kissing and hugging each other like there was no tomorrow.

'Excuse me? Hello, I'm here standing next to you hearing your smacks!' I didn't say this to them but I was tempted to.

Just what I needed on the way home. Nice!

Pride

It was gloomy and raining again this morning. It was quite depressing, to be honest.

When am I going to see the sun again? I don't like winter!

I was carrying a parcel on the way to work this morning. In it was a nice jacket that I used to love. Not anymore. I just sold it on eBay and had to post it this morning. Both my hands were already occupied and I had to get my morning Starbucks fix. I put the coffee in the carrier bag so I could still carry the jacket with the other hand. And of course, it spilled.

'Oh Renelo, what am I going to do with you, son?' this voice in my head laughing at me.

I looked outside the window train for a while. It was gloomy and I got really sad. So I looked back inside the train and I saw a cute girl. I stared at her, I mean glance. My mood started to change. I started to feel happy. Despite my glances, she didn't look back at me.

That's fine.

Then, I felt sad again.

On the tram on the way home, a guy told this pretty woman who just swiped her myki card that she didn't have to do it because we were in a free-tram zone. She said she was getting off anyway. She didn't say thanks to guy and she actually didn't get off. She just walked away from the guy to the back of the tram and stayed there.

The heck!

Pretty. Pride? Crazy!

3rd, Wednesday

Petals

I had five minutes to spare before my train arrived. I looked around and saw this first-aid girl. I believe a number of train stations have first-aid staff during peak-hour travels. I thank them for their time and dedication.

There were two medium size ladies sat on both priority seats facing each other. They were reading romance novels. There was obviously not enough room for me to sit on so I just stood in the middle of both of them and watch them read. I felt like I was as a pinch of salt in the middle of the twin towers. That's fine, I like towers.

They're like flowers without petals because I've eaten them.

I have no idea what that means.

4th, Thursday

Spanish

When I got out of Parliament Station, a young woman was handing out Review weekly magazines. She had the sweetest smile in the world. I took the mag and smiled back. This was the same girl whom I was supposed to give a love letter to but didn't happen.

I didn't make it happen. I couldn't. I got busy okay.

Then I thought about the wearables for singles business that I am working on. I could give the first product to her actually, instead of a love letter. Suddenly my emotions start running crazy. I then went to Starbucks to get my caffeine fix and continued working on the business plan.

As I was walking towards the tram stop after leaving work, I saw this girl shaking her body. I thought she was doing some Taylor Swift moves but as I got closer I realised she was shivering and was just trying to warm herself up. I initially thought about joining her so she could show me some moves. She might punch me in the head. It happened to me before so I better behave.

5th, Friday

Angel

It felt really good that it's Friday on a long weekend. It was so quiet on the train that I felt like I was on the island where Tom Hanks was trapped in the movie Cast Away.

When I was waiting for the tram to work, I saw an angel at the tram stop. She was the most beautiful thing I've ever seen. She had the cutest and bluest eyes.

Man, I could literally finish this business project I'm working on right now!

She stood at almost the height as me which is 165 centimetres. She looked really cute on her black trench coat. Our eyes locked for two seconds twice until someone started to talk to her. Then her tram arrived.

My heart broke at that moment.

6th, Saturday

No tram

I parked my car in Carlton and tried to catch a tram to the city. I found out later that there were tram works on Swanston Street. To have massive works on the main busy street in Melbourne is something that would inconvenience a lot of people particularly on a long Queen's birthday weekend. Well, I was one of them. I had to walk from Carlton to Bourke Street. I don't mind burning calories which is good for me but there was no notice that this was going to happen. Or maybe I just missed it. I would think that massive tram works like the one today would have plenty of notice. As you may already know I don't wear my eyeglasses to commute. I only use them when I drive.

I did a lot of walking today. Thanks to Yarra Trams. No, really, thank you! I'm not joking. I burned 97.77 calories today.

7th, Sunday

Brown hair

I did more walking again today and burned more calories. It looked like the tram works would continue throughout the long weekend. Well, it's good that they did this when most people are not at work. It's bad for those who wanted to go around Melbourne like the tourists.

I did some saxophone practice today at the studio. It was one of those sessions where I sax for one hour and you want to sax more but couldn't because you already scheduled other things to do. I practised for about an hour. I blew the last note on the sax and then started packing up.

I got on Tram 86 to the city and I saw another pretty girl.

Why are there so many pretty girls around here?

Anyway, the girl was wearing bright-coloured scarf and batik-styled dress. She has brown hair. I like brown hair.

9th, Tuesday

Red pants

I feel weird today that after a long weekend with my family, I have to go back to work but all I can think of is not to work.

I don't want to work! I want more time with my nephews and niece.

By the way, by family, I mean my sister, my brother and their kids, respectively. Every time I visit them, I feel the pressure to get married and have kids. That would be a separate 'love project' altogether. The only problem is, I don't even have a girlfriend. I'm just so occupied by my projects that if I start this *'love project'* now, it would slow the other projects down. Let's put it at the back-burner at this stage. I just hope it doesn't get burned there.

I'm wearing my red pants today. I feel weird that I'm wearing a pair of red chino pants. A little confident and at the same time embarrassed. I don't know how you chunk those two at the same time in your emotional tank but I just did. I feel unique that I'm the only one wearing this pair of red pants. I also feel that I'm out of place.

10th, Wednesday

Disappointed with my face?

When I got to the platform this morning I realised that I didn't put my moisturiser on. So just before swiping my Myki card to the platform, I ran back to the car to get my moisturiser. For me, it is the equivalent of make-up for women. I can't go to work without it. It's crazy! I don't know how I developed this habit, or shall I say, obsession. After putting some moisturiser on, I ran back to the platform like a cheetah. I made it to the express train!

Once on the train, I pulled out and put on my yellow earphones. For some reason I feel more confident when I use yellow earphones. I need to buy more of these earphones.

A cute girl working on her laptop put her head up and started to look around. That's when she saw me. When our eyes locked for two seconds, she looked down again and continued working on her laptop. I'm not sure if she was disappointed of what she saw or she just wanted to finish what she was doing. I'm confident that because I put some moisturiser on this morning that she wouldn't be disappointed with my face.

If my friends could hear my thoughts, they would just raise their eyebrows.

11th, Thursday

Good reflexes son

I got on the train this morning and noticed that everyone was standing. There was an empty seat but no one wanted it so I took it. I realised that the girl I sat next to had very drowsy eyes. She started to doze off. The next second I started dozing off too. I napped for a few minutes.

When I opened my eyes, I saw people getting off the train. So I got up and pushed my way into the exiting crowd. When I stepped off the train, I realised I was at the wrong station. It all happened so quickly that I barely had time to think. Though, I still managed to hop back on the train before the doors shut behind me.

'Good reflexes, son!' I thought.

A well-dressed man at the tram stop with a leg injury walked slowly past me. He had some style I must admit. He was wearing an expensive shiny leather brown shoe on his left foot and Nike runner on his right foot with tourniquet on his leg. I didn't know whether to laugh at his newly-discovered fashion or to feel sorry about his injured leg.

On the train home, I was on the phone with someone when the line was suddenly cut off. The train just entered the city loop. I was left with a situation whether to ring him back or wait for him to call me back. I ended up ringing him back.

My commute ended with a pretty girl getting off at Canterbury Station who gave me a big smile as she walked off.

Nice! I can sleep well tonight.

It's amazing how a simple smile can make someone's day or good night sleep.

12th, Friday

I will miss you

When I opened my eyes this morning, I looked at the clock and it was 7:26 A. M.

Crap, I forgot to set my alarm on last night. I probably won't get a car spot at the station.

I jumped out of my bed, washed my face and changed. All were done in seven minutes. Adrenalin kicked in. I must have been too tired that I just went straight to bed last night and completely forgot about the alarm. This happened to me a couple of times in the past. One of them was when I got back from Sydney to participate in a music festival. I couldn't sleep when we stayed at the festival accommodation. So I knew that after the event when I get home that my body needed to catch up.

I was out of the house by 7:35 A.M. and got to the station in five minutes. I found a spot for my car! I was extremely lucky to get a spot after 7:00 in the morning.

Or was it luck?

On the train home, this guy was eating his dinner in front of me. He had three pieces of sushi. He literally showed me how he chewed the sushi.

Unbelievable! What the heck? Just hearing the sounds of his chewing, I couldn't help myself visualising the inside of his mouth with _____ and _____ and a bit of soy sauce. Nice!

After listening to the sushi session, I continued reading the *mX* paper. It was the last issue of *mX*. I think they decided that it was too costly to run the paper based *mX* so they are moving online. While I was reading it, I noticed a few awkward messages, some of them rude. I suppose being the last issue, the care factor would almost be zero. I think they were previous censored messages sent to *mX* that they decided to publish in the last issue.

I'm sad. I will miss you, *mX*.

14th, Sunday

360 degrees

I sprinted to catch the tram to Melbourne Central. When I got on the tram, I could hear a loud girl's voice talking to someone in Spanish. I turned around and saw a _____ girl with curly hair and a 1960s pair of jeans. It made me think about *The Sound of Music* movie. Anyway, I thought she was talking about how she likes her housemate's friend that it caught my attention.

Then this older lady with shopping trolley got on the tram. She looked disoriented. She did a 360-degree turn and looked at everyone on the tram. Then she took a seat. At the next stop, she got up and hopped off the tram.

Interesting.

The Devil Wears Prada

Part of doing this book project was the hope that I will meet someone. Someone who can rock my world and make it more exciting. But it looks like nothing is happening and I'm the only one in my world. I need another rock.

Then my heart started to pound. It was not because of the pretty girl who was sitting next to me but because I was running late to the workshop that I had to attend. It started at 6:30 P.M. At 7 P.M. I was still on the tram.

Hurry up, tram!

Right after the tram stopped, I sprinted to what I thought was the workshop venue. I went to the wrong building. I was going in circles for a few minutes until I decided to ask some help. My phone has been playing up so I couldn't use Google Maps properly. I went into the building in front of me and I asked the receptionist for some directions. She told me to turn around because it was right behind me.

As I started walking I could see the building number and name of the building next door. It was my venue!

Embarrassing!

I went in the workshop room very quietly and tiptoed towards the very back. Still, three people managed to hear me. They turned around and gave me the look.

What?

The seminar was almost finished when I came in. The workshop finished on time. I spoke to a girl on the way out and she had been in public accounting practice for a number of years. I didn't get her number though.

Spewing!

I had to walk east and she was headed south.

I was pretty tired by the time I got to Flinders Street Station. I thought I'd take a nap. Before I closed my eyes, I saw this girl with long black shiny hair sitting on the priority seat. She looked like Anne Hathaway. It reminded me of the movie *The Devil Wears Prada*.

I decided not to take a nap.

16th, Tuesday

Sushi

Remember the girl who wore the same outfit for two straight days (see my entry called *Coloured* on the 27th of April).

Guess what?

She was there again this morning, on the same carriage I was on. To my surprise she was wearing a different outfit altogether. New black jacket, very light grey pants, grey pair of shoes, blue scarf with cream stripes and a pair of nice-looking pair of eyeglasses.

It started to rain while I was waiting for my tram to work. In the CBD area though, you can avoid getting wet by taking shelter from tram stops, walkways and buildings structures. I didn't need an umbrella. Well, I didn't bring it with me.

I was reading the paper when a girl sat on her luggage and started eating sushi. I got up and offered my seat to her. She didn't want it.

Okay fine! Enjoy your sushi.

The two ladies on their motorised chairs then started staring at me.

What now?

17th, Wednesday

The Rendezvous

I was running like crazy to make it to the train. Luckily, I didn't slip or anything. That's probably the worst thing that could happen to anyone—falling on the platform on the way to work, without dying of course.

I got on the train and the guy I stood next to was wearing rainbow socks while on his suit and tie. I noticed that this is becoming a trend now. I see them on corporate-dressed guys more than kids.

Does that mean adults want to feel like kids again?

While I was looking at his socks a girl was looking at my stomach. I don't know what's down there but I can assure you, there ain't no six-pack in there. I am no Dwayne Johnson.

What happened next on the tram was a little awkward because I thought I found my true love. A guy was sitting on my right. He seemed normal. He occasionally looked at his phone but mostly towards the front of the tram. He looked like he was waiting for someone. I looked at where he was looking and all I saw was the boring wall.

Okay, what is this guy up to?

While I was looking at the boring wall, a girl walked past the wall just behind the tram driver's cabin. She looked at her phone then continued walking towards my direction and stood next to me.

'Crap what the heck? Do I know this girl? She must know me,' I was trying to collect my thoughts and myself.

The next minute I realised she wasn't looking at me. She was looking towards the guy on my right. Then she started to walk closer towards the guy. She kissed him. They started talking. Then I realised they were a couple. The tram was their meeting place.

18th, Thursday

Dr John De Martini

My morning was greeted again by a cute *Review* magazine girl. The same girl who hands out magazines at Parliament Station every Thursday. As I towards them I could almost _____ her _____.

What? I said I could almost <u>read</u> her <u>lips</u>, say 'Thanks.' She always says 'thanks' every time I grab a copy from her.

'Hey, you brighten up my day every Thursday. My name is Ren. What's yours?' I was practising in my head.

As I walked closer she handed me a copy of the magazine but I couldn't open my mouth. I got tongue-tied. Another lost opportunity. Or was I just too shy?

Crap, what's happening to me? Why can't I do this? Someone please help me!

I went to work thinking what could have happened if did say those words. We could be sipping soy cappuccino at Grand Hyatt and enjoying barramundi fish and prawns at Vue De Monde. It's all but a dream now.

After work I went to John De Martini's inspiration speaking event called *Access Your 7 Greatest Powers* at the Melbourne Convention Centre. All these years that I thought only Austin Powers has them. Good to know that I can have some too.

When I arrived at the Convention Centre, it took me a lot longer to access the powers. I was late and I couldn't find De Martini. I didn't think he would be hard to find. I thought he would be more famous than that. I walked down the lobby and asked a well-dressed man with some sort of earpiece. I assumed he was security. He gave me directions:

'Go up, you'll see a big yellow door. You can't miss it. It's there.'

I followed his simple and exact directions. When I got up the stairs, there was no big or yellow door. How could I not miss something that is not even there in the first place?

I kept on walking, hoping to find some signs of De Martini and his followers. I couldn't find anything.

I was beginning to think the guy who gave me directions could be playing a trick on me and that there was not big or yellow door after all. So I decided to walk towards the other direction. Then a girl appeared all of a sudden, out of nowhere, while I was trying to look for this big, yellow door. I would describe her as having the same height as mine, a fellow De Martini supporter, a fellow late comer and perhaps a fellow soul-searcher. I started the conversation by asking her.

"Are you looking for De Martini event?"

"Hmmm, yes. I've been looking but I couldn't find any sign or anything." She said. "Let me check the venue again on my phone," she looked down on her phone trying to figure out how the heck we ended up here.

There were no signs or anything to point us in the right direction. We both tried to find the room. There were times she was following me but most of the time I was following her. I knew women are better at instincts.

"This way," she said.

"Okay," I replied.

After seven minutes of searching we finally found where it was. It was one level above us. We registered and went into the room. We were already late. De Martini was speaking and he saw us entering the room, he paused for a few moments. When we were sat, he continued talking. Thank you, John.

I caught the train after the event, with lavender. A passenger on the train opened a bottle of lavender and the whole carriage smelled lavender. All I could think about was all I could smell about—lavender. De Martini, gone.

19th, Friday

Likes

Almost everyone is using Beats by Dre headphones. Every time I see someone with a pair of headphones, I can almost predict that it would be a Dre. Even this man in his 60s standing next to me at the tram stop.

Now, I'm trying relax before my take-home examination is released at lunch time today. I have three hours to revel with. And I don't think going to work can be classified as revelling.

This outfit looks good on a Caucasian girl: Black beanie, black framed eyeglasses, purple scarf and brown hair. Try it. Assuming you have brown hair of course.

I didn't get her name and number.

A pretty girl gave her seat up for a disabled elderly woman who was sitting a few metres away. Good on you, girl. The ones closer to the woman didn't even move a muscle.

Another cute girl on the tram, although I must admit that she looked older that what she was. I don't know how old she is but estimate that if she doesn't frown she would look like 27 years old. I reckon a frown increases your age by at least 10 years.

On the way home, I continued reading a romantic, comedy book called *The Rosie Project* on the train. While I was reading the part where Don and Rosie, the couple in the book, were about to be engaged, I hear these two friends, a girl and a guy, talking about their families; the guy's father is a psychiatrist and his mother a teacher. His sister is a TV reporter in Tasmania. One thing I noticed or heard is this guy used the interjection 'like' a million times. Every other word is preceded by 'like.' I'm actually guilty of this too. *Like*, if I talk to someone *like* I know, *like* I feel *like* I belong to someone like no other place, *like* it's the best place. *Like* it's amazing *like...*

What the heck was all this?

20th, Saturday

Straight

I have a question for ladies: If a guy looks at you for at least 30 seconds, do you assume that he likes you? 30 seconds could be an exaggeration but hopefully you get my point.

Anyway, the reason I ask is because this morning, after a few minutes of looking around for things that I can jot down for my travel diary, my eyes got tired. So I decided to just look straight. That's it. No more moving of eyeballs. Just straight! And guess what was right in front of me? A woman's back. Not that I liked what I was seeing. I was just trying to look straight.

22nd, Monday

Gladiator

My tax take-home examination was due today all I could think of was whether it was good enough or not. I couldn't be bothered observing other people today on the train. I was still trying to collect my thoughts about two of the questions in my exam. You won't believe how much detail I had to go through the tax legislation just to prove a point or two. Capital gains, main residence exemption, profit-making undertaking, roll-overs, CGT events, etc. I'm making you bored right now. I know. Yes, that's what I had to deal with for four months.

Then this Renaissance-looking guy gets on the train. He looked overly serious. He was wearing a Renaissance-looking design on his trench coat. It reminds me of Commodus, that cruel emperor played by Joaquin Phoenix, in the movie *Gladiator*. That guy who fought Russell Crowe in a duel

I felt a little sleepy on the train to the city this morning. I tried to wake myself up by walking up the escalator really fast. All of a sudden, a girl in her gym outfit overtook me. She was almost running. I was tempted to overtake her.

I thought if I do it, it wouldn't be a very 'gentleman' thing to do.

So, I didn't overtake her.

23rd, Tuesday

Snot super dry

This guy standing next to me was picking his nose. He then rubbed his snot between his thumb and index finger. Once transformed to a diminutive matter, he then rubbed it on his light-coloured pair of jeans creating a nice little black smudge. I just stood there dumbfounded. I actually thought I didn't need my caffeine fix this morning. This was enough to wake me up.

On the train home, I was sitting opposite a tall girl who was sitting with crossed legs. I was reading my book when my butt became itchy. I didn't really want to scratch my butt in front of the girl so I tried to fight back. Itch is evil. After a few moments, I couldn't hold it anymore so I copied the girl. I crossed my legs and discreetly scratched my behind. The evil was defeated with finesse.

24th, Wednesday

Love story

I have been thinking a lot about the book I started reading recently. Somehow, I forgot about the world around me that I felt like was part of the story I was reading.

I tried to look up to rest my eyes from reading. Then, I saw a pretty girl. It felt like staring at a painting without frames. Again, I felt like I was part of the love story I was reading. At this point, there was little or no difference between the girl on the train and the girl in the story.

That's what happens when you read too much romantic comedy stories, folks.

25th, Thursday

Who's sheepish?

I didn't hand the love letter to the Spanish girl this morning because of one problem – I didn't do it.

She handed me a copy of this week's Review magazine at Parliament Station. I was kicking myself inside for not writing the letter last night.

Shall I say it to her instead? What if she rejects me? What the heck? I should have prepared the letter. Why is this happening to me?

26th, Friday

Cupcakes for sale?

I was looking out the window while the train was moving. When the train stopped at Camberwell Station, right in front of me. I saw a big billboard of a girl pointing her right index and middle fingers to her forehead which looked like the letter 'F' to me. On her forehead were three big letters **U C K**. Was she trying to swear at me?

Was she really meant to do that? What product was she trying to sell? Cupcakes? I don't think I'm going to buy her cupcakes. Besides, I had enough sweets this week. I need something spicy.

27th, Saturday

No girlfriend, buddy?

I caught a tram from Carlton to the city to my hairdresser. A guy sitting opposite me looked very sad. I knew why.

Do you want to know why?

Scroll down to see.

He doesn't have a girlfriend. Don't worry buddy. I don't have one either.

29th, Monday

Go away!

I couldn't decide whether to do some work at my local cafe or go to the city. So I walked around the train station for a bit, towards the platform then back to the car park. Indecision hit me today. It's ridiculous. Go away!

I caught my train to the city and then my tram to work. I got off the tram a few stops before my usual one so I could walk. While I was walking, I saw a pair of abandoned black leather shoes on the footpath. Unfortunately, they weren't my size.

I did a lot walking this morning. Indecision, thanks but no thanks.

Romance

I have just finished reading a romantic comedy book called *The Rosie Project*. I don't know why I was so eager to finish it. When my nephew first showed it to me, I was sceptical. I mean I could watch romantic love movies but I didn't think I could read books about them. My nephew showed me a couple of reviews and when I got home I also checked out more reviews about them. They were all great reviews. So I took action. When I got on the train the next day I started reading it. Later, I realised that it was going to completely ruin my schedule for the next few weeks. All my weekly routine and plans for the next two weeks were out the door. The first two chapters got me hooked. It completely entertained me.

I love it.

Rosie, it's all your fault! I'm not talking to you anymore! Go away!

I also need to tell you one thing. After finishing the book, I received a message from a dating site I signed up for ages ago. When I read the message I saw that it was from a woman in Queensland. At first, I hesitated to read it. I was a little bit uncertain about these sorts of things online because lately I've been hearing things about people pretending to be someone else using other people's photos. I managed to overcome my scepticism and eventually I opened the message.

I thought it was love.

I was wrong.

JULY 2015

1st, Wednesday

Secret Service

Four men in suits surrounded me on the train. I don't think they were the US Secret Service. I'm pretty sure Obama didn't fly out of America today. So there wouldn't be any reason for the Secret Service to be here.

Anyway, I didn't mind if they wanted to protect me. That's fine.

2nd, Thursday

Joining the conversation

I was holding and eating a wafer stick like a cigarette while waiting for my train. I was basically emulating a smoker using a wafer stick. While I was doing this, I noticed a lady was watching me. So I quickly swallowed my smokes. I mean wafer stick.

Then I got on the train. She jumped on the train too, just behind me.

Why is she following me? What the heck? She must be a smoker or something. Smokers attract smokers. But I'm not! I'm a wafer stick smoker.

I recently got hold of the sequel of the book that I just finished reading called *The Rosie Project*. The second book is called *The Rosie*

Effect. I knew I was going to get hooked on this romantic comedy crap. It's ridiculous. Anyway, I wanted to start reading it this morning on the train but I could hardly move. I was standing in the middle of the crowd and I couldn't reach a rail to hold onto. I didn't want to fall and embarrass myself with a romantic comedy book all over the floor.

On the way home, a guy was talking loudly on the phone. Everyone could hear him. He was saying how everyone on the train was wearing leggings. It was obviously an exaggeration. Then this girl sitting next to me who was wearing a pair of khaki leggings, raised her left leg to show the guy on the phone. Then she laughed. Everyone on train laughed.

The guy was on the phone for ages. He was also telling the person on the other line not to steal their friend's puppy bells.

3rd, Friday

Rosie Effect

On the way to work this morning, I continued reading Graeme Simsion's book *The Rosie Effect* on the train. I got hooked on this Rosie romantic comedy series. It's crazy. There's something magical about it. Every time I read it on the train, I feel like in a different world. It's just full of fun, excitement and unpredictability.

Don Tillman, the main character in the book, is somehow influencing the way I think. He has Asperger's syndrome. He is very analytical even with the smallest of things. He would explain the principles behind things and events.

On the way home this evening, I continued reading the book again until I got hungry. The tram being late didn't help. I was growing impatient.

Where the heck is this tram? I need food. Don Tillman, wait for me!

5th, Sunday

The best way to wake up someone on the train

I was looking around the carriage when I noticed a medium size man who was two seats away from me. He had a very serious face. It wasn't not a normal serious. It was weird serious. After a couple of moments, I realised why he looked that way.

While I was sitting there dozing off, he made a very loud sneeze that it work me up.

What the heck was that?

I was wide awake after that. Thanks man.

6th, Monday

Miscommunication

I was rushing to catch my morning train. I made it but I was gasping for air when I got on the train. The doors closed but the train didn't move. After about thirty seconds, it looked like something was wrong but there was no announcement or notification. Two minutes passed and still no notification. Finally, a station staff announced that the train was not taking passengers and advised us to board the other train from the other platform.

We all jumped out and moved to the other train. When the train started to move, we realised that the train was stopping at all stations to the city. The Metro staff didn't say this when he made the announcement. I could have just waited for the next express train instead. It was too late to change. At least, they could have said that the train would stop at all stations and what time the next express train would arrive to give commuters options.

I was disappointed at how they handled the communication this morning. It felt angry when an express train went past us.

I continued reading *The Rosie Effect* to divert my attention and ease my emotion.

Rhyme!

7th, Tuesday

Love and hate

For some reason I caught the same train I caught yesterday. When I say same, it means the same departure time. This was despite the train stopped at all stations to the city. It didn't make sense. Not at all!

Why is it that sometimes, we attract or do the things that we hate? I reminds me of love stories of people who ended up marrying they hated or disliked. Can someone please give me a psychological or scientific explanation to this?

On the way home, I was trying to remember all the girls I've known in the past that I disliked. 'The One' could be one of them. Perhaps, this 'love-hate' theory may apply to me.

8th, Wednesday

Online dating

I met a girl online called _____. What happened was I signed up for a Christian dating website that I heard being advertised on the radio. I've always been sceptic about online dating. I've been sceptic for too long without a valid reason that I decided to challenge my scepticism. So I decided to join the website.

I didn't get any results for some time so I didn't log in for a while and stopped updating my profile. That was until I received a message one day from this woman. We exchanged messages. And that's how it all started.

I've been thinking about her lately. In fact, she's always on my mind that sometimes, I lose my concentration.

9th, Thursday

Awkward situations

The one thing that I like about winter is wearing fashionable jackets, jumpers and coats. I was excited yesterday to wear one for today.

However, I couldn't find my favourite jumper last night. I spent at least an hour looking for it but to no avail.

Guess what?

I found it this morning while putting on my top.

Success!

Sometimes if we just sleep over our problems we find the answers when we wake up the next day. I think I read a book about subconscious mind that if we let our subconscious mind explore solutions to our problems, we would be amazed at how far it can go.

Two girls and a guy were talking in a different language while I was standing right in the middle of them. It sounded Indonesian. The tram was packed so it was bit hard to move so I was stuck there listening to their conversation that I could not understand.

I was rushing to get home after work so I ran from the tram stop to Southern Cross Station. A medium size lady with her luggage next to her was on the escalator when I was running up the escalator. I could see there was small gap between the handrail and her luggage. I estimated the gap to be seven inches. I took it and managed to squeeze in, touching the lady's luggage. I made it to the train with 60 seconds to spare. I looked back and smiled at the lady while I was about to hop on the train.

I was trying to say sorry.

10th, Friday

Tax

After a couple of months' break from radio, I came back to talk about tax. The financial year has just ended and people started to get their tax returns done. It was great to be back at the studio and see my fellow broadcasters again. It was a little bit out of my way but it was worth it.

While waiting for my train this morning, I heard some private conversation over the intercom. For a moment, I thought an announcement was being made for train passengers. Then, I realised a staff had the intercom on while he was having a private conversation with someone. I wouldn't like to be in that position.

No, thanks.

The conversation was very interesting that I couldn't help myself listening to it. I actually missed my train because of that. I had to wait for the next one.

The conversation was about _____.

Secret!

11th, Saturday

Saturday special AKA work

I compiled some of the train travel entries from 2014. I brought my nephews with me to Gloria Jeans to help with the editing. I think kids and teenagers have far better ideas than adults sometimes. I get more ideas from them in just a day than anywhere else. You just need to guide them by asking the right questions. I needed ideas on how to present the travel entries. We spent three hours at Gloria Jeans then we drove to the city. We caught the tram to Starbucks to continue our work. They realised their myki cards were running out of credits and we were about to board the tram.

We shot some videos at Starbucks for YouTube. People gave us a nasty look.

What are you looking at? Just mind your own business.

12th, Sunday

Gloves

I caught the tram on a freezing early Sunday morning to South Melbourne. I hesitated at first because it was so cold but the more I think about whether to go or not, the more time I wasted. In the end, I just packed my things and went. It's not productive to think too much about little things.

I caught the tram home. Luckily, I brought a pair of gloves with me. That's probably one little tip I can give you when you catch the public transport in Melbourne in winter—a pair of gloves. I recently bought a few pairs and put one pair in each of my jackets and jumpers. I don't need to worry about forgetting them.

I was preparing to get off the next stop when an elderly man got up and started walking towards me.

'What the heck? What's going on here? Did I do anything wrong or what?' *I was freaking out* and didn't know what to do.

Meanwhile, he was getting closer. I was tempted to walk away but for some strange reason, something is telling me to wait for him. He tapped my shoulder and pointed to the floor. It was my left pair glove. I picked up it said thanks to him.

I was relieved.

13th, Monday

High heels

I bought a good pair of men's leather high heels on the weekend. I wore it today to work. For the first and the last time. They look amazing but they're just too uncomfortable on my feet.

I wonder how ladies do it. High heels to work every day. I wouldn't last half an hour. And women's heels are a lot higher than men's.

I felt like going home and change my shoes.

Going home again just to change shoes? Nah.

I suffered today. Heeled shoes, you're the culprit!

14th, Tuesday

Insomnia

I couldn't sleep properly last night. Crazy heeled shoes!

I remember my mother used to say to me that if you can't sleep, just close your eyes and rest.

And that's what I did last night.

The next morning when I got up, although I felt I didn't have sleep, I rested at least.

On the train to work, I was standing and looking blankly at people like a zombie.

On the train home, I also stood the whole time until I got home. I felt a little bit better compared to this morning.

15th, Wednesday

Greased lightning

I felt a lot better when I got up this morning compared to the previous day. That meant only one thing—I had a good sleep last night.

I was singing on the train. I didn't care. I had to celebrate.

I was able to do quite a bit on my website while sipping coffee at Starbucks this morning. I was in the mood that I almost missed my tram. When I realised that my tram was just outside the cafe, I closed my laptop, slipped in my bag and ran. The tram has just closed its doors.

Crap! I have to wait for the next one! Ridiculous.

While I was standing there frustrated, someone got off the tram. In a split second, I sped towards the door like a lightning and jumped on board.

I made it!

I continued reading *The Rosie Effect*.

16th, Thursday

!Xobile and Russell Peters

I got on the train and heard someone talking on the phone with a Jamaican accent. Then, I remember Russell Peters, a famous comedian from Canada. In one of his shows, he talked about how he met a Jamaican guy named !Xobile. At first, he was wondering how to pronounce it because of the exclamation mark at the beginning that he saw on his name tag. He thought he needed to put a bit of emotion while saying the name so he sort of yelled at the guy. Then the Jamaican guy told him not to yell. So Russell asked him how to say his name. Then the guy said the exclamation mark is a click. So it is pronounced as CLICK-o-bee-lay.

YouTube it — Russell Peters Jamaican names.

17th, Friday

Nothing

I don't want to talk about what happened today.

20th, Monday

Hanging over my shoulder

On the train on the way home, I was reading my tax exam results when this very tall guy leaned over the wall divider with his hands touching my shoulder and exam booklet. He seemed oblivious of what he was doing. And I almost going to erupt.

Nice! Just nice! Just what I need on a Monday night. Calm down Renelo!

Luckily, I did calm down.

No sweat has spilled today.

21st, Tuesday

Resume

I was enjoying reading *The Rosie Effect* book when this guy got on the train to the city and shoved his butt into the gap between me and the wall. He did not say a word. He pulled out some papers out of his leather laptop bag and started reading them. It was someone's resume.

First of all, no commuter courtesy. Second, a resume contains private information and should be read in public places where other people can see.

Anyway, I didn't say anything to this guy. I just gave him a look once in a while but that was about it. I wanted to send him a message about what he was doing. He didn't get the message.

22nd, Wednesday

Handbag

I was standing on the train on the way home when this lady next to me started touching my butt with her handbag. I didn't know if it was intentional or not. I never experienced this before in my years of catching the public transport. I didn't know what to do.

After about two minutes that this was happening, I decided to push her handbag gently away from me.

Guess what?

It didn't work!

What the heck?

I started walking towards the back of the train away from her.

23rd, Thursday

CBS

Today is one of those days. You know, those CBS (can't be stuffed) days. I got up a little bit late than normal. I was lucky to still get a car spot at 7:15 A.M.

Or was it luck again?

After work, I dropped by the hairdresser to get a haircut. I felt good after that. That's probably the only thing that made me feel good today. Nice.

24th, Friday

My ever dearest saxophone

A schoolboy on the train was carrying an instrument. I'm pretty sure it was a trumpet based on the shape and size of the bag. By this time, I already had put the saxophone project on hold. This travel diary book project is taking a lot of my time so I need to focus on this first. After this book is published, I will continue my saxophone lessons. Sometimes you need to delay your passion and address pressing matters. I consider this book a pressing matter. You know that.

To my ever dearest saxophone:

I miss you a million times to the moon and back and a day with salt and pepper. I will see you in a year or two. I can't wait to see you again! I want to touch your bell like never before. I want to caress your shiny, golden body while I fix your neck. I want to blow your mouthpiece for hours. I will never stop until I get tired. You are one of a kind. Mwah!

27th, Monday

Minority Report

Melbourne is full of weird guys. I got on the train this morning and right beside me was *The Blue Green Man*.

Seriously!

He was wearing a glittery green cape. He held a green umbrella with his right hand. Unfortunately, he had blue headphones on. He was holding a blue bag as well.

While I was reading on the tram, at least four myki ticket inspectors got on board and started asking people to show their myki cards. The whole scene was very similar to a particular scene in the movie Minority Report where the pre-crime police officers released the electronic spiders to look for Tom Cruise who was on the run for committing a future crime that was fabricated. Anyway, the spiders function like a miniature police eye-scanner to identify the people in the perimeter. Whatever you are doing, you must stop and let them scan your eyes or there will be consequences. This was how they try to catch a fugitive. Fortunately, Tom Cruise had replaced his eyeballs with someone else's.

On the way home, the train had a defective sign that I wasn't sure if I was jumping on the right train. The monitor that showed the scheduled trains was also not working. So the train driver was bold enough to get out of his cab and shout:

'Lilydale, Lilydale train. Lilydale, Lilydale train. It's not Glen Waverley. It's Lilydale, Lilydale train!'

I felt like I was at Victoria Market on a quiet Sunday morning.

28th, Tuesday

Overtake

As soon as I parked my car I ran towards the platform to make it to my train. My train was due in two minutes. A man in front of me was so slow that I had to overtake him. I had no choice. He gave me a nasty look.

Fine. Sorry.

Take it easy. Okay?

Just relax a little bit.

29th, Wednesday

The other Green Man

The last time I saw *The Blue Green Man*, he was wearing a green cape and had a green umbrella. This time he had a green hair. The colour wasn't that obvious so I wasn't looking at him all the time. I wasn't distracted at all. I wasn't completely affected.

I'm joking.

Of course I looked at him. In fact, I stared at him. I don't think having a green hair is something you can hide on the train. I tried not to stare but I just couldn't help myself. He saw me looking at him so I tried to look away. Once he wasn't looking I looked at him again.

How can you not look at him? He's *The Blue Green Man.*

He didn't seem to know where he was going because he tried to get off the tram a few times.

He would look around every time the tram stops and probably thought: 'Nah this is not my stop.'

Well, where is it?

30th, Thursday

Vandalism

There were serious train delays this morning.

Not happy Jan!

The train staff announced that the trains have become defective after some people broke into the depot and vandalised the trains.

I don't what's happening to the world. It's has gone mad. Absolutely crazy! This was not the only time. I heard similar stories in the past and it just blows my mind why people do those things.

31ˢᵗ, Friday

Happy Financial New Year!

As the last day of the financial year, I had to buy a few things so I could claim them on my tax return. I was either checking the ATO website to verify some information about claims or reading a few tax books.

I thought about making today as the last day of entry on my train travel diary because it's the last day of the financial year. It's been a long project so far, having to compile daily entries from September 2014 until now.

We'll see how we go tomorrow.

Lessons learned

To finish on the last day of the financial year symbolises both and end and a beginning for me. I continued taking travel notes until the end of September 2015 out of habit. I stopped after that. I stopped because I realised that it was not entirely me who was taking those travel notes. It was the Renelo that was forced to complete a project

It's an end to a project that took my freedom to be myself. I forced myself to be someone I'm not. It's like locking yourself up in a room for almost a year without internet. I don't like watching other people's activities on the train. I certainly don't like to listen to other people's conversations.

The completion of this project also marks the beginning of a new Renelo. During my journey, I became more observant to little things, sensitive to quiet conversations and easily distracted by pretty women. As I began to realise what the project was transforming me into, I thought about giving up towards the end of the project. In fact, I thought about it quite a lot that I couldn't sleep for some nights. In the end, I decided that I didn't want to break the promise I made to myself. I stuck to the initial plan and completed the project.

I realised that because of this book project, I discovered more things about myself that I would not have known otherwise. I realised that I have more discipline than I thought. I learned how to appreciate beauty in its true sense, not as a result of testosterone. I learned how to be more considerate to other people. I developed incredible levels of patience and forgiveness during my journey and towards the completion of this project.

Lastly, I discovered more of my weaknesses as a human being. I was guilty of pointing out other people's shortcomings that I overlooked my own. I realised that people are quick to judge or label other people just because they are different, both in physical features and ideology.

I am not perfect. I made mistakes. I know.

I'm a better person because of this project.

HAPPY COMMUTING!

Check us out on:

www.trainconfessions.com

ww.facebook.com/confessionsofamelbournecommuter

www.instragram.com/renelodrummer

Printed in the United States
By Bookmasters